African Americans in Early North Carolina:

A Documentary History

To be SOLD at Edenton, on Monday the 2d of November,

SUNDRY likely NEGROES, Men and Women; a BRIG about eighty Tuns Burthen, with all her Materials as she came off a Voyage from Jamaica, eighteen Months old, and well calculated for the Navigation of this Part of the Province, draws nine Feet Water full loaded, and may be sent to Sea at a small Expense; also a Quantity of good barrelled HERRINGS, being Part of the Estate of the late Richard Brownrigg. The Terms of Sale ready Money, and Discount of any Debts due from the Estate, as the Executrix and Executors then intend to settle and pay off all just Debts. The Inventory of the Brig to be seen any Time before the Sale, at Mrs. Brownrigg's, and at John Campbell and Son's Houses; where any Person inclining to buy the Brig at private Sale may be treated with, and know farther Particulars.   (1 1)

Newspaper advertisement announcing sale of "SUNDRY likely NEGROES, Men and Women." *Virginia Gazette* (Williamsburg: Purdie and Dixon), October 22, 1772.

The Colonial Records of North Carolina
Special Series
Jan-Michael Poff, Series Editor

African Americans in Early North Carolina:

A Documentary History

Compiled and Edited by
Alan D. Watson

Office of Archives and History
North Carolina Department of Cultural Resources
Raleigh
2005

Cover: Runaway slave advertisement from the *Wilmington Centinel, and General Advertiser*, June 18, 1788.

Printed by Edwards Brothers Inc.

www.ncpublications.com

Contents

Foreword

The state of North Carolina has been publishing its early documents since 1886, when the first of ten volumes of the *Colonial Records of North Carolina*, edited by William L. Saunders, was produced. Almost 80 years later, in conjunction with the 300th anniversary of the Carolina Charter, the current or Second Series of published colonial records was inaugurated. These two complementary collections, containing transcripts of thousands of original documents on the founding and development of the colony, have proved invaluable to scholars who explore and interpret North Carolina history.

To introduce North Carolina's documentary heritage to a broader audience, Robert J. Cain, editor of the *Colonial Records of North Carolina [Second Series]* and head of the Colonial Records Project of the then Division of Archives and History, envisioned a new "Special Series" of soft-cover titles. Each book in that new series would feature selected records addressing a specific topic. The first of these soft-cover editions, *Society in Early North Carolina: A Documentary History*, was released in 2000. Although Cain was describing *Society* in particular, his statement from the book's foreword summed up well the design for the entire Special Series of the *Colonial Records of North Carolina*: "It is intended to be of interest to a wide range of readers, suitable for the classroom and indeed anyone curious about the lives of North Carolinians as recorded by the colony's citizens and visitors during the earliest years of its history."

Alan D. Watson, who so ably compiled and edited *Society in Early North Carolina*, brings this latest title, *African Americans in Early North Carolina: A Documentary History*, to the Special Series. Drawing upon a variety of seventeenth- and eighteenth-century sources, ranging from private correspondence to legislation, he outlines the arrival of Africans, mechanisms for maintaining the yoke of slavery, slave resistance, manumission, and the challenges facing free blacks in the colony and state through 1800. Watson's commentary, introducing and joining together thematically grouped excerpts from North Carolina's written past, is set in bold type. As reproduced herein, the documents themselves retain the spelling, capitalization, and uses of italics, punctuation, and numbers that appear in the originals.

A prolific author, Watson is professor of history at the University of North Carolina at Wilmington and vice-chairman of the North Carolina Historical Commission.

Jan-Michael Poff, Series Editor

Acknowledgments

I extend my deepest appreciation to Jan-Michael Poff, Head, Colonial Records Project, and his staff for their transcription of documents, editorial contributions, and general preparation of this volume for publication. Theirs was tedious, laborious, behind-the-scenes work that too often goes unrecognized, and yet was indispensable in bringing this project to fruition. In particular I would like to thank Robert J. Cain and Dennis L. Isenbarger for proposing several documents that have been included in this compilation. Last, I am grateful for the assistance of many librarians and archivists, who go unnamed but who also helped to make this volume possible.

Alan D. Watson

Introduction

The African American experience in North Carolina, as in the rest of European America during the early modern age, proceeded from a tragic, forced enslavement of African peoples to a life of bondage in the New World. Although a few African slaves resided in western European countries before 1500, the Portuguese, in their successful quest to find a water route around Africa to the Indian Ocean and the Indies in the mid-fifteenth century, inadvertently opened the possibility of an extensive commerce in humans. The western European countries needed little additional labor, for many deemed themselves over-populated at the time. Yet within fifty years, Columbus opened the Americas to colonization. As the Europeans began to assume control of the American continents, they found an abundance of land but a scarcity of labor. At first they resorted to the forced servitude of Native Americans, but soon began to substitute Africans for Indians as slaves.

The land that became North Carolina early may have witnessed the temporary presence of Africans as the Spanish, from their colonies in the West Indies, explored and even attempted a settlement along the Atlantic coast in the 1520s. After the passing interest of the Spanish and the voyage of Giovanni da Verazzano, who sailed for France and reached North Carolina in 1524, Europeans showed little concern with the area until the abortive English settlements under the auspices of Walter Raleigh in the 1580s. Raleigh's colonists did not include Africans; but when Sir Francis Drake visited Roanoke Island, his huge fleet included African slaves whom he had liberated from the Spanish in the West Indies and promised freedom. As he prepared to take Raleigh's colonists back to England in 1586, Drake released the Africans along the North Carolina coast to an unknown fate.

Africans only reappeared in North Carolina following the permanent settlement of the region in the late 1650s. Virginians and other immigrants brought limited numbers of blacks as slaves to the colony in its formative years. By 1700, African Americans numbered approximately 400, amounting perhaps to 4 percent of the total population. Their numbers rose significantly during the eighteenth century, comprising an ever-increasing proportion of the total population, until they constituted perhaps a quarter of all North

Carolinians at the beginning of the American Revolution. The federal census of 1800 found 140,339 blacks living in North Carolina, at that time 29.4 percent of the state's populace. Their presence was most pronounced along the coast, particularly in the Lower Cape Fear, and in the north-central area bordering Virginia.

Immigration and natural increase explained the growing number of African Americans in North Carolina. Although the Outer Banks rendered seaborne trade difficult, including that involving slaves, ships still brought small cargoes of slaves to the ports of Edenton, Bath, Beaufort, and New Bern. In the southeast, where the Cape Fear River flowed directly into the Atlantic, slaves were more easily imported into Brunswick and Wilmington. At the same time, as the number of slaves increased, individual slaveholdings enlarged; the sex ratio achieved greater parity, families formed, and natural reproduction augmented and eventually overtook immigration as the principal source of blacks in North Carolina. A true African American population arose after 1808, when Congress, under Article I, Section 9 of the United States Constitution, outlawed the foreign slave trade.

The institution of slavery in North Carolina evidenced four basic characteristics: racial identification, lifetime status, bondage of offspring, and chattel property. As property, slaves constituted particularly valuable assets whose labor was virtually requisite to the accumulation of significant wealth by whites. Nonetheless, they were human, people who struggled against mighty odds to cope with the trauma of enslavement in Africa, the shock of transportation to America, and the oppression and degradation of bondage in North Carolina. In the process, they interwove native Africanisms with their new American experience to produce a Creole culture that revolved around family, religion, and work experience. Some were fortunate eventually to obtain their freedom when their owners liberated them, usually for meritorious service, but also, in the case of Quakers, because of a growing moral opposition to slavery.

As the slave population increased, the North Carolina General Assembly passed several laws, collectively called a "slave code," to regulate and restrict the actions of bondsmen. For guidance and precedent, the legislature often depended upon the slave legislation of Virginia and South Carolina. Still, blacks ignored the laws, often with impunity and to their peril. Although the slave code was aimed primarily at blacks, it placed restrictions on whites as well, because the legislature wanted to prevent both sexual and commercial intermingling of the races. Again, neither blacks nor whites well observed the legal strictures, for human desire and pecuniary gain overrode statutory enactments.

Slaves exhibited their opposition to bondage in various ways. From obstinate behavior, to petty theft, to felonious crimes, they challenged the slave code. Most were disciplined by slave owners. Those committing felonies might be tried in slave courts, legally sanctioned judicial bodies that possessed plenary powers of investigation and judgment. In addition to the slave courts, the slave patrol represented the principal means by which white society attempted to maintain control over slaves. The patrollers searched the living quarters of slaves for weapons, apprehended runaways, guarded against insurrections, and in general enforced the slave code. Still, the patrol, like the slave courts, proved less than fully effective in intimidating or restraining the actions of slaves.

Unable to endure their bondage, countless slaves ran away, and some even threatened to engage in insurrection, though such organized action never materialized in North Carolina. Runaways, whether recent arrivals or long-time inhabitants of North Carolina, departed singly and in groups. A few looked for temporary respite from the rigors of slavery; most sought permanent freedom. The arrival of the British military in North Carolina during the American Revolution offered an immediate opportunity for some slaves to obtain their freedom by fleeing to British lines. Otherwise, runaways tried to make their way to safety in nearby colonies or states, took surreptitious passage by boat from North Carolina, or hid in inaccessible areas such as swamps, where their presence was difficult to detect and dislodge.

Although most North Carolina slaves, like whites, resided in rural areas, a few appeared in the small urban communities of the colony and state. In the towns, slaves undertook menial public and domestic work; in the seaports along the coast, they also toiled in the maritime trades as sailors, pilots, and stevedores. Urban slaves seemed to enjoy considerable latitude as attested by numerous legal measures designed to restrict their activities. Some owners allowed their bondsmen to hire their services in return for a stipulated payment. With their compensation, slaves occasionally rented dwellings, in effect living independently of their masters. On other occasions, slaves were left in charge of town homes while their owners resided on plantations during part of the year.

While the vast majority of African Americans in North Carolina at the beginning of the nineteenth century were slaves, a small but growing number of free blacks and mulattos appeared in the colonial era and the years of the early republic. That number was comprised of emancipated slaves, runaways who claimed to be free, children of white women whose fathers were slaves or free blacks, and free black immigrants from other colonies. In 1800, North Carolina's 7,043 free African Americans constituted 5.3 percent of the state's black population, but only 1.5 percent of the total population. Relatively few lived in towns: 144 in New Bern, 67 in Fayetteville, 19 in Wilmington, and 18 in Raleigh. Free blacks in North Carolina suffered from legal discrimination, though many led lives resembling those of average non-slaveholding whites. Nonetheless, their color set them apart, and their greatest apprehension was enslavement or re-enslavement by unscrupulous whites.

This documentary attempts to trace the history—the travails, the hopes, the triumphs—of African Americans, slave and free, in early North Carolina to the end of the eighteenth century. A variety of sources have been used to exemplify the richness of the materials available for the study of North Carolina history. Always important were the provincial and state laws, for laws reflected the norms of society, in this case those of the ruling whites, most of whom were slave owners. However, the manifold deviations from the statutes or norms betrayed the efficacy of laws to control the behavior of African Americans, both slave and free. Indeed, while the words of blacks, as interpreted and transcribed by whites, appear infrequently, their actions along with the ever-present restrictive and punitive legislation spoke loudly on behalf of their efforts to create a place for themselves in North Carolina under adverse circumstances.

Slavery and the Slave Trade

The Fundamental Constitutions, a document drafted in 1669 by the Lords Proprietors of Carolina for the governance of Carolina colony, recognized and encouraged slavery. White immigrants registered members of their families, and their slaves, in order to claim headrights, or land grants, from the government.

101. Every Freeman of Carolina shall have absolute Authority over his Negro Slaves, of what opinion or Religion soever.

Fundamental Constitutions, 1669, in Mattie Erma Edwards Parker, ed., *North Carolina Charters and Constitutions, 1578-1698*, Volume I of *The Colonial Records of North Carolina* [*Second Series*], ed. Mattie Erma Edwards Parker, William S. Price Jr., and Robert J. Cain (Raleigh: Division of Archives and History, Department of Cultural Resources [projected multivolume series, 1963-], 1963), 150.

North Carolina SS.   To the Honorable Generall Court
    Mr. Jno. Durant humbly Sheweth that he hath right to one hundred acres of land by importation of Sampson [and] Ruth Negroes which he is ready to prove and craves certificate and shall etc. pray.

John Durant

General Court, April-June 1697, in Mattie Erma Edwards Parker, ed., *North Carolina Higher-Court Records, 1697-1701*, Volume III of *The Colonial Records of North Carolina* [*Second Series*], ed. Mattie Erma Edwards Parker, William S. Price Jr., and Robert J. Cain (Raleigh: Division of Archives and History, Department of Cultural Resources [projected multivolume series, 1963-], 1971), 72.

The slave population of North Carolina rose rapidly during the eighteenth century. Natural reproduction accounted for much of the increase, which was augmented further by the immigration of slaveholding whites and the burgeoning slave trade. Some Africans were brought overland from neighboring Virginia and South Carolina. Others entered North Carolina as part of the colony's seaborne trade with mainland English colonies, particularly Virginia and South Carolina, and the West Indies. Still others were imported directly from the Guinea Coast of Africa, which extended from present-day Guinea-Bissau to Nigeria.

LIEUTENANT GOVERNOR BENJAMIN BENNETT TO THE BOARD OF TRADE.

BERMUDA, August 4, 1708.

[. . .] That about 36 years agoe (as I am Inform'd) a small ship (her name nor Capt's. remembred), went from hence to Callebar on the Coast of Guiny, and brought back One hundred twenty five negroes, near half of whom were disposed off here (but att what prices I cannot learn) the rest were reshipt for Carolina and Virginia. Also abt 25 years since, Another ship went from hence to Callebar, Comanded by one Capt. Stone (her name not remembred) and brought back abt Ninety slaves: But most of them was carry'd to North Carolina, Virga, and placed on the Continent, and there disposed off, but att what rates can't be informed. [. . .]

Elizabeth Donnan, ed., *Documents Illustrative of the History of the Slave Trade to America*, 4 vols. (1931; reprint, New York: Octagon Books, 1965), II:48. Calabar is located on the coast of present-day Nigeria.

Since our last, the schooner Joseph, Capt. Williams, arrived here from Barbadoes, with a Parcel of fine healthy young Slaves; [. . .]

North Carolina Magazine; or, Universal Intelligencer (New Bern), September 21, 1764.

Newbern, December 20, 1774.

Just imported in the SCHOONER HOPE,
Thomas Foster, *Master, from* AFRICA,
A Parcel of likely healthy

SLAVES,

Consisting of Men, Women, and Children, which are to be sold for Cash, or Country Produce, by EDWARD BATCHELOR & Co. at their Store at UNION POINT.

North Carolina Gazette (New Bern), January 13, 1775.

[. . .] No Negroes are brought directly from Guinea to North Carolina, the Planters are obliged to go into Virginia and South Carolina to purchase them where they pay a duty on each Negroe or buy the refuse distempered or refractory Negroes brought into the

Country from New England and the Islands which are sold at excessive Rates.

George Burrington to the Commissioners of His Majesty's Customs, July 20, 1736, in William L. Saunders, ed., *The Colonial Records of North Carolina*, 10 vols. (Raleigh: State of North Carolina, 1886-1890), IV:172.

The *NEGROES* are sold on the Coast of *Guinea*, to Merchants trading to those Parts, are brought from thence to *Carolina*, *Virginia*, and other Provinces in the hands of the *English*, are daily increasing in this Country, [. . .]

John Brickell, *The Natural History of North Carolina*, (1737; reprint, Murfreesboro, N.C.: Johnson Publishing Co., 1968), 272.

The importation of slaves continued until the American Revolution, when the colonials adopted measures to end the practice. Rowan County residents expressed their opposition to the "African Trade" in August 1774, a position assumed later that year by the First Provincial Congress of North Carolina and the First Continental Congress. When slaves continued to arrive after the non-importation deadline of November 1, 1774, set by the Continental Congress, the Wilmington-New Hanover Safety Committee required that the bondsmen be reshipped from North Carolina.

Proceedings of the Freeholders in Rowan County

AUGUST 8th 1774.

At a meeting August 8th 1774, The following resolves were unanimously agreed to. [. . .]

Resolved, That the African Trade is injurious to this Colony, obstructs the Population of it by freemen, prevents manufacturers, and other Useful Emigrants from Europe from settling among us, and occasions an annual increase of the Balance of Trade against the Colonies.

Saunders, *Colonial Records*, IX:1024, 1026.

THE JOURNAL OF THE PROCEEDINGS OF THE FIRST PROVINCIAL CONVENTION OR CONGRESS OF NORTH CAROLINA, HELD AT NEWBERN ON THE TWENTY-FIFTH DAY OF AUGUST, A.D. 1774.

[. . .] Resolved, That we will not import any slave or slaves, nor purchase any slave or slaves imported or brought into this province, by others from any part of the world after the first day of November next.

Saunders, *Colonial Records*, IX:1041, 1046.

THE ASSOCIATION [OF THE CONTINENTAL CONGRESS]

October 20, 1774 [. . .]

2. We will neither import nor purchase, any slave imported after the first day of December next; after which time, we will wholly discontinue the slave trade, and will neither be concerned in it ourselves, nor will we hire our vessels, nor sell our commodities or manufactures to those who are concerned in it.

Henry Steele Commager, ed., *Documents of American History*, 2 vols., 7th ed. (New York: Appleton-Century-Crofts, 1963), I:84-85.

WILMINGTON, SATURDAY THE 17TH OF DECEMBER, 1774.

The committee met according to adjournment.

Present: Corn's Harnett   John Ancrum   Rob't Hogg
    Arch'd Maclaine   James Walker   John Robeson
                                             John Quince

The committee finding upon Inquiry that one of the slaves Imported by Herreld Blackmore was ordered after the Publication of the Resolves of the provincial convention of this province, and in contradiction thereto, and that he had at that time an opportunity to contradict the Orders he had given for the other Slaves, and he now confessing that he sent a coppy of the provincial resolves to Granada — It is the opinion of the committee that the said slaves be reshipped. And the committee do resolve that all slaves Imported since the first day of this Instant, or which may be Imported, shall be reshipped from this province.

Leora H. McEachern and Isabel M. Williams, eds., *Wilmington-New Hanover Safety Committee Minutes, 1774-1776* (Wilmington, N.C.: Wilmington-New Hanover County American Revolution Bi-Centennial Association, 1974), 5.

The slave trade in North Carolina resumed after the Revolution. One of the largest shipments of Africans occurred in the mid-1780s as a result of the formation of the Lake Company, which proposed to dig a canal from Lake Phelps, in present-day Washington County, to the Scuppernong River in Tyrrell County. The General Assembly, in 1786-1787, tried to restrict the trade in slaves by levying a tax on those imported by land or water, an action that inflicted economic hardship on Henry Hill and Thomas Fitt, who in 1788 petitioned the state House of Commons for relief. Subsequently, in 1790, the General Assembly repealed the law.

[Edenton, June 10, 1786]. Mr. [Nathaniel] Allan has a brig arrived today from the coast of Guinea. She has only been seven months on her passage out and home and has a hundred slaves aboard in the state of nature (women and men). They talk a most curious lingo, are extremely black, with elegant white teeth. They shipped corn to Guinea, which turned out to a great profit, and the Negroes at twenty-eight pounds sterling by that means did not stand them in near the money. They are all from twenty to twenty-five years of age. Mr. Allan has bought them to drain a lake on the other side of the sound (which was discovered about thirty years ago) by digging a canal seven miles long. He expects to finish it by Christmas if it ceases raining [. . .] in keeping 150 slaves daily at work. The expense, he says, will be £3,000 at least, but when the work is accomplished he will have cleared 100,000 acres of the finest woodland that almost was ever known (oak, sycamore, poplars, cypress, etc.) — which is an amazing object and a very great undertaking. [. . .]

Louis B. Wright and Marion Tinling, eds., *Quebec to Carolina in 1785-1786. Being the Travel Diary and Observations of Robert Hunter, Jr., a Young Methodist of London* (San Marino, California: Huntington Library, 1943), 267.

CHAPTER V.

An Act to Impose a Duty on all Slaves Brought Into This State by Land or Water.

Whereas the importation of slaves into this State is productive of evil consequences, and highly impolitic:

I. Be it therefore Enacted by the General Assembly of the State of North Carolina, and it is hereby Enacted by the authority of the same, That from and after the passing of this Act, a duty of fifty shillings per head on all slaves under seven and over forty years of age, and a duty of five pounds per head on all slaves between the ages of seven and twelve years, and between the ages of thirty and forty years, and a duty of ten pounds per head on all slaves of twelve years and upwards to the age of thirty years, shall be collected by the collectors of the different ports in this State, on all slaves brought into any of the said ports; which duty shall be collected and accounted for in the same manner, and under the same regulations as are prescribed for collecting and accounting for the duties on goods, wares and merchandize, &c. imported into this State.

Laws of North Carolina, 1786, in Walter Clark, ed., *The State Records of North Carolina*, 16 vols. (11-26) (Raleigh: State of North Carolina, 1895-1906), XXIV:792-793.

FRIDAY, 21 November, 1788.

The House met according to adjournment. [. . .]

The Committee to whom the Petition of Henry Hill and Thomas Fitt was referred, Reported,

That the said Petitioners had at a Considerable expence & risque fitted out a ship to Coast off Africa for a Cargo of Slaves; That at the time the said Ship sailed the duty on imported Slaves was no more than two and a half per cent.; that after the sailing of the said ship and before her return the Law was passed increasing the duty on Slaves imported from Africa and that the Petitioners, ready to make every compensation in their power, are willing to pay double the duty which was laid on Slaves at the time they commenced the said voyage. Your Committee are therefore unanimously of opinion that the said Petitioners on paying double the duty receivable on slaves on the first day of October, 1786, that is to say on their paying five per cent. on the original cost of the said Slaves, they be exonerated from the payment of any other or further duty on the said cargo of slaves imported from Africa some time in May or June, 1787, and that the collector of the Imports for Port Roanoke Govern himself with respect to the said Cargo or Slaves accordingly.

All which is submitted.

THOMAS PERSON, Ch'n.

The House taking this report into consideration concurred therewith.

House Journal, 1788, in Clark, *State Records*, XXI:75, 82.

CHAPTER XVIII.

An Act to Repeal, [. . .] One Other Act Passed at Fayetteville, in November, in the Year One Thousand Seven Hundred and Eighty-Six, Entitled, "An Act to Impose a Duty on all Slaves Brought Into This State by Land or Water. [. . . "]

II. And be it further enacted by the authority aforesaid, That so much of the before recited Act imposing a duty on slaves brought into this State by land or water, be and the same is hereby repealed.

Laws, 1790, in Clark, *State Records*, XXV:80.

———————

As a reaction to the successful slave insurrection of 1791 in Sainte-Domingue, the General Assembly imposed a substantial fine on those who imported slaves into North Carolina. Adopted in 1794 in an attempt to halt the slave trade, the legislation made exceptions for slave owners from the United States or foreign countries who intended to reside permanently in the state, those traveling with slaves through North Carolina, and persons who inherited slaves from out-of-state. In 1795, the legislature specifically forbade whites emigrating from the West Indies, Bahamas, and southern Atlantic coast from bringing adult slaves into North Carolina. Later that year, several gentlemen from Jamaica fruitlessly petitioned Benjamin Smith, speaker of the state senate, for an exemption from that law. But the General Assembly subsequently

made an exception for Archibald Campbell, who already resided in North Carolina.

CHAP. II.

An Act to prevent the further importation and bringing of slaves and indented Servants of colour into this State.

I. BE *it enacted by the General Assembly of the State of North-Carolina, and it is hereby enacted by the authority of the Same,* That from and after the first day of May next, no slave or indented servant of colour shall be imported or brought into this state by land or water; nor shall any slave or indented servant of colour, who may be imported or brought contrary to the intent and meaning of this act, be bought, sold or hired by any person whatever.

II. *Be it further enacted by the authority aforesaid,* That every person importing or bringing slaves or indented servants of colour into this state after the said first day of May next, by land or water, contrary to the provisions of this act, shall forfeit and pay the sum of one hundred pounds for each and every slave or indented servant of colour so imported or brought. [. . .]

Laws of the State of North-Carolina, 1794, c. 2.

CHAP. XVI.

An Act to prevent any person who may emigrate from any of the West-India or Bahama Islands, or the French, Dutch or Spanish Settlements on the Southern coast of America, from bringing Slaves into this State, and also for imposing certain restrictions on free persons of colour who may hereafter come into this State.

I. BE *it enacted by the General Assembly of the State of North-Carolina, and it is hereby enacted by the authority of the Same,* That from and after the first day of April next, it shall not be lawful for any person coming into this state, with an intent to settle or otherwise, from any of the West-India or Bahama Islands, or the settlements on the southern coast of America, to land any negro or negroes, or people of colour, over the age of fifteen years, under the penalty of one hundred pounds for each and every such slave or persons of colour, to be recovered before any jurisdiction having cognizance of the same, one-fifth to the use of the informer, and the other four-fifths to the use of the state.

II. *And be it further enacted,* That it shall be the duty of such person or persons bringing in any such negro or negroes, or people of colour, under the age of fifteen years, to prove the age of the same by his own oath, or the oath of some other person, before some Justice of the Peace, if the same be required.

Laws, 1795, c. 16.

Dear Sir,

There is a Sloop arrived in this port in great Distress from the Island of Jamaica, on board of which are about nine or ten Gentlemen of respectibility, besides their wifes and Children, they have on board between 30 and 40 slaves, which have been ever Faithfull to them, and have followed their masters where ever they went.

Some of the above Gentlemen have been prisonners of war on their parole in Jamiaca for upwards of 20 months. A late proclamation in the Island of Jamaica, has been put in force for all French people to take oath of Allegiance and to bear arms in the British Service against their own Countrymen or Else to quit the Island, the above Gentlemen of Course prefered the latter, and they obtained passports from the British Gouvernment to retire.

These Gentlemen in their present Distressed situation, wish to become Citizens of the united states and to make this one their place of residence and to be allowed to land their negroe slaves which they have no intention of disposing of, T[hey] beleive the laws of this state is in their favour, but a Town meeting which was held this day has given them some uneasiness apprehending that they will not be admitted as Such, and that some steps are taking to prevent the Landing of their slaves. I therefore come to Request you in behalf of these Gentlemen to lay their Case open to the honorable Assembly in Case it should be deemed needfull and I have no doubt but what it will take their deplorable Situation into Consideration. I remain most respectfully Dear Sir your very humble servant

P Manyeun
deputé agent of the French Republic

Letter from the deputy agent for the French Republic, resident in Wilmington, to Benjamin Smith, December 2, 1795, Slave Collection, State Archives, Office of Archives and History, Raleigh.

CHAPTER LXXIII.

An Act for the relief of Archibald Campbell.

WHEREAS Archibald Campbell, a native and citizen of this state, by the will of his late uncle Archibald Campbell, of the Island of New-Providence, one of the Bahama Islands, hath become entitled to, and possessed of sixty negro slaves; and hath represented to this General Assembly his intention to use the work and labour of said slaves on his lands in Orange county, where he hath generally lived and now resides.

I. *Be it therefore enacted by the General Assembly of the State of North-Carolina, and it is hereby enacted by the authority of the Same,* That the said Archibald Campbell be permitted and authorized to import and bring into this state, the said negro slaves, or any part thereof: any law to the contrary in any wise notwithstanding. *Provided nevertheless,* That the said Archibald Campbell shall by the testimony of two or more creditable persons, taken by and before authority competent thereto in the island of Providence, ascertain and substantiate what negroes were devised to him by the last will and testament of his uncle and identify the negroes by particular description, to the end those alone may be imported into this state by virtue of this act; and further prove by testimony taken as aforesaid, that the said negroes, describing and identifying them, be not slaves captured by privateers and sold in the island of Providence, or elsewhere in the Bahama or West-India islands, or have been concerned in any insurrection against the government.

Laws, 1799, c. 73.

Slaves: Property, Labor, and Emancipation

Slaves represented a most valuable form of property in early America. Bondsmen were not only the most important marker of social prestige, but through their labor offered the principal avenue to material wealth. Those touting the benefits of North Carolina — like "Scotus Americanus," prospective immigrant Franz Ludwig Michel, resident James Murray, and Governor William Tryon — recognized the advantages of slave ownership. Seth Pilkington, a wealthy Beaufort County merchant and planter, had acquired twenty-six slaves by the time of his death.

[1773]. Young healthy negroes are bought there for between 25 and 40 l. Five of these will clear and labour a plantation the first year, so as you shall have every thing in abundance for your family, with little trouble to yourself, and be able to spare many articles for market; [. . .]

Scotus Americanus, "Informations Concerning the Province of North Carolina, Etc.," in "Some North Carolina Tracts of the Eighteenth Century," ed. William K. Boyd, *North Carolina Historical Review* 3 (October 1926): 615.

I have seen several examples, among the others I will tell you of a man named Puis from home who arrived here two years ago with nothing. [. . .] Last year he made by his own effort 45 pistoles from rice without counting the other products and from this money he bought two black slaves with whom he made 80 pistoles from rice this year; according to all appearances, in a short time, this man will be a gentleman of ease. [. . .] All of this only approaches the profit which may be made in this land. [. . .] But it is necessary to remember that one does not have everything without hardships or care. One cannot have them without some capital, in spite of which he must work himself for one cannot have servants in this country where every one is rich. One employs slaves, and though they seem to be expensive, they are always considered to be much better than the servants in Europe, being more submissive and more robust for work, and one feeds and clothes them as one finds proper.

Franz Ludwig Michel to "My brother" [Hans Ludwig Michel], February 20, 1703, in Géza Schütz, ed., "Additions to the History of the Swiss Colonization Projects in Carolina," *North Carolina Historical Review* 10 (April 1933): 134-135.

JAMES MURRAY TO WILLIAM ELLISON

BRUNSWICK, 14th Febry, 1735/6.

DEAR SIR—

[. . .] I intended to have gone up to New town, Alias New Liverpool, but was told there was no house there to be had except I built one; so was oblig'd to bring all ashore here, where I have got a good convenient house on rent, which I shall keep until I can purchase a few slaves & a plantation in the country where I can have all kind of provisions of my own raising. [. . .]

Nina Moore Tiffany, ed., *Letters of James Murray, Loyalist* (Boston: the editor, 1901), 24. New town is modern-day Wilmington. Murray rented his home from Roger Moore, one of the wealthiest landowners in the colony.

[. . .] [July 26, 1765]. The Negroes are very numerous I suppose five to one White Person in the Maritime Counties, but as you penetrate into the Country few Blacks are employed, merely for this Simple reason, that the poorer Settlers coming from the Northward Colonies sat themselves down in the back Counties where the land is the best but who have not more than a sufficiency to erect a Log House for their families and procure a few Tools to get a little Corn into the ground. This Poverty prevents their purchasing of Slaves, and before they can get into Sufficient affluence to buy Negroes their own Children are often grown to an age to work in the Field. not but numbers of families in the back Counties have Slaves some from three to ten, Whereas in the Counties on the Sea Coast Planters have from fifty to 250 Slaves. A Plantation with Seventy Slaves on it, is esteemed a good property. When a man marries his Daughters he never talks of the fortune in Money but 20 30 or 40 Slaves is her Portion and possibly and agreement to deliver at stated Periods, a Certain Number of Tarr or Turpentine Barrels, which serves towards exonerating the charges of the Wedding which are not grievous here.

William S. Powell, ed., "Tryon's 'Book' on North Carolina," *North Carolina Historical Review* 34 (July 1957): 411. Tryon based his conclusions on slavery from a tour he took of the colony between December 1764 and February 1765.

INVENTORY of the Estate of Seth Pilkington Decsd taken by
Michl Coutanche Feb. 27th 1754. [. . .]

Negroe Men
   Jupiter, Lankeshire, Catto
   Darby, Cudgo, old Tom
   young Tom, Jack, Pomp,
   Fortune, George, Dublin,
   Noridge
Negro Boys
   Mustifer, Cain, York,
   London, Bristol,
Wenches
   Africa, Grace, Jenny Flora
   old Betty,
Girls
   Jenny, Pheby, Hannah, [. . .]

Inventory of Seth Pilkington, in J. Bryan Grimes, comp., *North Carolina Wills and Inventories*
(Raleigh: Edwards & Broughton Printing Co., 1912), 525, 528.

**Thus whites to their advantage bought, sold, and hired African
slaves as they did inanimate forms of property, including ships
and fish. As Peleg Greene discovered, sale depended upon
market conditions, including the availability of slaves and the
terms of credit. The auction block witnessed the shame and
degradation of blacks, and often led to the separation of families
despite entreaties to the contrary. Auctioneers made extravagant
claims to inflate the value of slaves, but bondsmen, if possible,
just as assiduously denied them. Spared the trauma of sale to
"Strangers" and alienation from loved ones were a number of
elderly slaves belonging to Sir Nathaniel Dukinfield, who were
purchased by Samuel Johnston and Penelope Dawson.**

To all People to whome this presant Bill of sale shall come, John
Butler of Onslow County and Province of No Carolina Send Greeting
Know thee that I the Said John Butler for and Consideration of the sum
of Fivety Pounds Proclamation Money to me in hand well and truly
paid at or before the Ensealing and Delivery of these presants By

William Jameson of Said County and Province aforesaid Merchant the Receipt whereof I do hereby Acknowledge and am therewith fully and enterely Satisfied and contented Have Granted Bargained and Sold and by these Presents do grant Bargin and Sell unto the said William Jameson a Negro Boy named Arthur To Have and to hold the Said Granted and Bargained negro Boy unto the Said William Jamieson his Heirs Executors Administators or assigns to his only proper Use Benefit and Behoof forever and I the said John Butler do avouch my Self to be the true and lawfull Owner of the said Negro and have in my Self full power, good Right and lawful Authority to dispose of the said negro Boy in manner as aforesaid. [. . .]

John Butler (Seal)

Deed of Sale, November 8, 1763, Onslow County, Miscellaneous Records, Slave (Bills of Sale), State Archives, Office of Archives and History, Raleigh.

To be SOLD *at* Edenton, *on* Monday *the* 2d *of* November,

SUNDRY likely NEGROES, Men and Women; a BRIG about eighty Tuns Burthen, with all her Materials as she came off a Voyage from *Jamaica*, eighteen Months old, and well calculated for the Navigation of this Part of the Province, draws nine Feet Water full loaded, and may be sent to Sea at a small Expense; also a Quantity of good barrelled HERRINGS, being Part of the Estate of the late *Richard Brownrigg*, [. . .]

Virginia Gazette (Williamsburg: Purdie and Dixon), October 22, 1772.

PELEG GREENE TO AARON LOPEZ

Newbern, No. Carolina, Sept. 13, 1772.

[. . .] The Negros I received at Jamaica all got in in good Health only Homer had two bad Places on one of his Thighs which wood not heal up but in Good Health other ways but however no[ne] of them fetch as mush I expected by reason of many cuntry born Negros was sold at Vandue and at Six months Credit which makes a great ods but however I have sold four of them named as follows —

Jack . . . . at 70

Cudjo . . . . at 70
Homer . . . . at 50
Newbuary Boy . . . . at 57:10 [. . .]

Commerce of Rhode Island, 1726-1800, Volume I, *1726-1774*, in *Collections of the Massachusetts Historical Society*, 7th ser., Volume IX (Boston: the society, 1914), 413-414. Prices are in pounds and shillings.

[Wilmington, January 1784]. Other negroes were sold and at divers prices, from 120 to 160 and 180 Pd., and thus at 4-5 to 6 times the average annual hire. Their value is determined by age, health, and capacity. A cooper, indispensable in pitch and tar making, cost his purchaser 250 Pd., and his 15-year old boy, bred to the same work, fetched 150 Pd. The father was put up first; his anxiety lest his son fall to another purchaser and be separated from him was more painful than his fear of getting into the hands of a hard master. "Who buys me, he was continually calling out, "must buy my son too," and it happened as he desired, for his purchaser, if not from motives of humanity and pity, was for his own advantage obliged so to do. An elderly man and his wife were let go at 200 Pd. But these poor creatures are not always so fortunate; often the husband is snatched from his wife, the children from their mother, if this better answers the purpose of buyer or seller, and no heed is given the doleful prayers with which they seek to prevent a separation.

One cannot without pity and sympathy see these poor creatures exposed on a raised platform, to be carefully examined and felt by buyers. Sorrow and despair are discovered in their look, and they must anxiously expect whether they are to fall to a hard-hearted barbarian or a philanthropist. If negresses are put up, scandalous and indecent questions and jests are permitted. The auctioneer is at pains to enlarge upon the strength, beauty, health, capacity, faithfulness, and sobriety of his wares, so as to obtain prices so much the higher. On the other hand the negroes auctioned zealously contradict everything good that is said about them; complain of their age, longstanding misery or sickness, and declare that purchasers will be selling themselves in buying them, that they are worth no such high bids: because they know well that the dearer their cost, the more work will be required of them.

Johann David Schoepf, *Travels in the Confederation, 1783-1784*, 2 vols., trans. and ed. Alfred J. Morrison (Philadelphia: W. J. Campbell, 1911), II:148-149.

June 30th, 1789

Dear Sir, [. . .]

With regard to my Legacy I should have been indifferent but I have paid one half of it to Mr. Iredell which it may be inconvenient for him to refund and I purchased three of the old Negroes beside Toney who importuned me with tears streaming from their Eyes not to let them fall into the hands of Strangers, pleading their long and faithfull Service to their Mistress and that they were wore out with Labour. This added to the entreaties of my Sister Iredell and some other of your Brother's friends prevailed on me to purchase them, tho they are rendered almost altogether useless by their age and infirmities and I was in no want of hands. The Negroes I purchased were London Bet and Suckey. Mrs. Dawson purchased Mars who begged that he might not be parted from his Wife and Children, he was quite worn out and died a few months after. [. . .]

Samuel Johnston to Sir Nathaniel Dukinfield, June 30, 1789, Hayes Papers, Southern Historical Collection, Manuscripts Department, Wilson Library, University of North Carolina at Chapel Hill.

Hiring out slaves was so advantageous to slave owners and non-slave owners alike that the practice was widespread. It permitted slave owners, both individuals and businesses like the Chatham Furnace, an iron-making facility in Chatham County, to utilize fully their bonded labor. At the same time, slave hire offered those who needed labor, including non-slave owners, access to that resource. It also provided flexibility to executors and administrators of estates and guardians of orphaned children in meeting their responsibilities. However, slave owners required contractual protection to guard against runaways and injuries or death occasioned by improper treatment of their property; and given the shortage of money in North Carolina, those who hired slaves were more likely to receive payment in kind than in cash. From the standpoint of the slave, hire, like sale, produced a separation of families and apprehension, if temporary, of a new master.

Acct. of the Negro Women

Milley and 2 Children hired to Martin Kindreck near the Forge

Patty and 1 Child hired to Malcolm Sinclair the Collier at the Furnace

Grace and 3 Children gone to Major Philip Alston

Pegg Lives with Colonel Ramsay

A Girl Named Jenny lives at John Thompsons on Deep River

A Lad Named Billey lives with Mr. Giffard at Cross Creek. [. . .]

James Mills to "Sir" [Archibald Maclaine], March 25, 1777, Chatham Furnace Papers, Southern Historical Collection, Manuscripts Department, Wilson Library, University of North Carolina at Chapel Hill. The furnace was located on Tick Creek.

After this, negroes were let for 12 months to the highest bidder, by public cry as well. A whole family, man, wife, and 3 children, were hired out at 70 Pd. a year; and others singly, at 25, 30, 35 Pd., according to age, strength, capability, and usefulness. [. . .] Whoever hires a negro, gives on the spot a bond for the amount, to be paid at the end of the term, even should the hired negro fall sick or run off in the meantime. The hirer must also pay the negro's head-tax, feed him and clothe him. Hence a negro is capital, put out at a very high interest, but because of elopement and death certainly very unstable.

Schoepf, *Travels in the Confederation*, II:147-148.

I do promise to pay John Lewis his Heirs Executors Administrators or Assigns the Sum of Eight hundred weight of Crop Tobacco or hard Mony at the Market price at Petersburg the tobacco if pd. to be Delivered at Petersburg for the hire of One wench and Two Children which Said Slaves is to be will Clothd and the Taxes pd. on Each, and Delivered with the Tobacco or Money the 17th day of January 1783 To which payment will and Truly to be made I do bind myself my Heirs Executors Administrators and Assigns in the Final Sum of Sixteen hundred weight of Crop Tobacco.

Saml. Hammond (Seal)

Signed Sealed and Delivd
in presence of
John <*his mark*> Horvel

Contract for slave hire, c. 1782, Granville County, Miscellaneous Records, Miscellaneous Records of Slaves and Free Persons of Color, State Archives, Office of Archives and History, Raleigh.

Abner Neale to John Gray Blount

MILE END April 4th. 1790

Sir/

Agreeable to our Conversation when at your place I attended at Mrs. Blackledges Vendue and hired Joe with his Wife and two small Children at forty Barrells Corn P year pay able on the 1st. day of January yearly and am to have them for three Years provided the Old Lady lives so long which I think there is no dainger but she will, I have also all the Tanners & Curryers Utensils which she had, on loan to be returned in kind and like good order, at the expiration of his time [. . .]

Alice Barnwell Keith, ed., *The John Gray Blount Papers*, Vol. 1, *1764-1789* (Raleigh: Division of Archives and History, Department of Cultural Resources, 1952), 37. Mile End probably was located near New Bern.

[. . .] [Edenton]. The profits of the plantation are much easier realized than the Negroe hire, where a man hires out his own Slaves and barters their Wages for Necessaries <*and Conveniences*> for the use of himself and family it turns out very well but when he expects Money it is quite different for of all the Credits I have given you for Negro hire I dont think I ever recd. £ 50 in Money. [. . .]

Samuel Johnston to Thomas Barker, June 10, 1771, Hayes Papers, Southern Historical Collection.

Slave labor contributed mightily to the development of North Carolina's economy in the eighteenth century. African Americans tilled the fields and worked the "turpentine forests." Slave artisans — coopers, nailers, and printers among many others — were indispensable as were musicians, particularly fiddlers, whose talents were so necessary for the dances enjoyed by blacks and whites alike. Females were utilized as house servants, though in small families like that of James Auld, they also worked in the fields. Childbearing, as noted by John F. D. Smyth,

interfered little with their routine. And women, as well as men, toiled in such industrial settings as the Chatham Furnace.

[July 26, 1765]. I suppose you will expect to be informed what return is Made for the expence of Supporting such a Number of Slaves in the Province. Their chief employ is in the Woods & Fields, Sowing, and attending and gathering in the Corn. Making of Barrels, Hoops, Staves, Shingles, Rails, Posts and Pails, all which they do to admiration, Boxing of Pine Trees to draw off the Turpentine, Making of Tarr kills [. . .]

Powell, "Tryon's 'Book'," 411.

THIS is to give all Persons Notice, that there is a Negro Fellow named HOLLOW, detained from me; he is about 30 Years of Age, a short well set Fellow, has a scald Head, is a good Cooper, likewise a Corker, and is a sensible Fellow. [. . .]

BENJAMIN BLOUNT.

March 10, 1775.

North Carolina Gazette (New Bern), May 5, 1775.

[*William Blount*] *to John Gray Blount*

PHILADELPHIA, August 11th 1787

I yesterday wrote and forwarded by post to you a letter on the Subject of making Nails and the Advantages of employing Negroes at that Business [. . .]

It has appeared to me that this Business of Nail making is a Business better calculated than any others for the Employment of Negroes and that it is among the most profitable of Businesses, your man Pollypus and my man Will I suppose would readily make as good Nails as any body [. . .]

Keith, *Blount Papers*, I:334-335.

RUNaway, about 6 Weeks ago, a Negro Man named Richmond, about 3[0] Years of Age, and about 5 Feet 5 Inches high; he speaks fast and but indifferent English. He belonged formerly to Mr. BARNHILL of Philadelphia, pretends to be free, and has been accustomed to a Printing Office; [. . .]

Cape Fear Mercury (Wilmington), November 24, 1769.

RUN AWAY from Mount Pleasant estate, on the North-West, a Negro fellow named TONY, late the property of Miss Cobham, well known in and about Wilmington, as he was one of the fiddlers to the assemblies. He is tall, well made, and thin vissaged, between black and yellow. He took away a fiddle, some carpenters tools, &c. [. . .]

GOODIN ELLETSON,

At Mount Pleasant, on North-West of Cape Fear,
Bladen, May 17, 1788.

Wilmington Centinel, and General Advertiser, June 18, 1788.

[. . .] in 71 hired no hands made about 30 Barrells of Corn with one old Fellow and help of the house Wench the other old fellow dying in the Winter past in Nov. 70. [. . .]

Entry of March 14, 1767, "The Journal of James Auld, 1765-1770," *Publications of the Southern History Association* 8 (July 1904): 262.

The female slaves fare, labour, and repose, just in the same manner [as the male slaves]; even when they breed, which is generally every two or three years, they seldom lose more than a week's work thereby, either in the delivery, or suckling the child.

John F. D. Smyth, *A Tour in the United States of America*, 2 vols. (1784; reprint, New York: Arno Press, 1968), I:47.

First I shall begin with Informing you how the Negroes are disposed of and how they Are Employd that Are here or at the Forge
Sambo is a Carpenter, and is manning the forge which last week, Capt. [Rowan Fargo], he, and Major Alston were fishing in, in a canoe, a Blessed place to make Barr Iron into Especially as it is frequently so.
Mingo Carts Coal, at the Forge, and a Boy named Toney leads the Oxxen.
Cuffee Tends the Forge with Coal etc.

Old Peter keeps the Mill at the Forge
No. 4 Men and 1 Boy at the Forge

at the Furnace

Julius the Smith
Sandy his Smiter, who also sometimes Stocks Coal
George Tends the Saw Mill
Doctor is Removing Rubbish from the Furnace and has been making Coal baskets
Jemmy
Peter   are with the Stone Cutter helping him to get Hearth Stones
Bristol
Sam   are always at Work with Malcom Sinclair the Collier
Toney
Cazar
Jacob   are Cutting Cord Wood here
Africa
Davy   is, and I believe always will be Lame, and can't do any work
13 men at the Furnace
4 men at the Forge
17 men which is All the Men
Sam and George Are Two Boys that Cart Coal at the Furnace
When the Furnaces is in Blast George assists in Keeping her, then the Saw Mill must Stand at All times, Except in a Fresh. [. . .]
Edey Cooks at the Furnace
Darkey her Daughter help her, her Other Children are a Charge. [. . .]

James Mills to "Sir" [Archibald Maclaine], March 25, 1777, Chatham Furnace Papers, Southern Historical Collection.

Slaves proved adept as watermen in America, operating ferries, guiding rafts and flatboats along rivers, and serving as pilots. Those occupations provided them with a responsibility, freedom, and association with whites unavailable to most bondsmen. White pilots at Ocracoke, however, complained about the competition offered by slaves and free blacks. But the need for pilots became so great that the General Assembly, in 1800,

permitted the licensing of slaves provided that their masters posted bond for their proper behavior.

[. . .] when I preach at Brunswick and in travelling to the different places where I am called or officiate have spent in the last two years about two hundred pounds this currency besides being often obliged to take two negroes for three or four days in a week to transport me by water where I necessitated to preach, [. . .]

> Rev. Richard Marsden to [Edmund Gibson, bishop of London], July 7, 1735, in William L. Saunders, ed., *The Colonial Records of North Carolina*, 10 vols. (Raleigh: State of North Carolina, 1886-1890), IV:12.

April 6, 1797

Ten Dollars Reward.

RAN away from the subscriber, a negro man call ANDREW, he is a stout thick set short fellow, about 24 years of age, remarkably dirty and slovenly in his general appearance, his hair thick, short and matted, and tho' a country-born, I question if it was ever combed; he has small eyes and thick blubber lips; the fellow was raised at the plantation that Mr. McGuire lived at, on the North-West, and it is possible he will harbour between that and Gen. [Thomas] Brown's, as he has a negro woman of the General for a wife; tho' it is more probable he may be taken lurking about Fayetteville, as he was accustomed two years ago to row in the boats that ply between Wilmington and that place. Whoever will apprehend said negro and deliver him at my plantation, or to the goaler in Wilmington, shall have the above reward paid them by

JOHN HILL

April 6.

> Advertisement in *Hall's Wilmington Gazette*, in Freddie L. Parker, ed., *Stealing a Little Freedom: Advertisements for Slave Runaways in North Carolina, 1791-1840* (New York: Garland Publishing Co., 1994), 127.

To His Excellency Josiah Martin Esquire, Captain General, Governor and Commander in Chief in and over the Province of North Carolina,

The Petition of Legal Pilots of Oacock Bar Humbly Sheweth that your Petitioners under the Sanction of an Act of Assembly of this Province have Settled at Oacock Bar in order to attend and Carry on the Business of their Calling at Great Costs and Expence as well for the Benefits Resulting thereby as for the advantage of Mariners and Traders of the Province in General

Notwithstanding which Sundry Negroes as well free men as Slaves to a Considerable Number by unjust and unlawfull means take upon themselves to pilot Vessels from Oacock Bar up the several Rivers to Bath, Edenton and New Bern and Back again to the Said Bar to the Great prejudice and Injury of your Petitioners Contrary to Law and against the Policy of this Country and to Trade in General

Your Petitioners therefore humbly begg Leave to Observe to your Excellency that the Pilotage at the said Barr at present no ways answer the salitary Ends Intended by Law as Great Confusion and Irregularity daily Insue from the Insolent and Turbilent disposition and behaviour of such Free negroes and Slaves

Under those Circumstances Your Petitioners humbly pray Your Excellency would please take this matter into Consideration And prevent the Like for the Future by denying License or Branch to any such Free negro or Slave Whatsoever

And Your Petitioners as in Duty Bound will Ever pray &c

JOHN WILLIAMS	ADAM GASKINS
GEO. BELL	RICHARD WADE
JOHN BRAGG	WILLIAM STYERIN
WILLIAM BRAGG	SIMON HALL.

Petition, undated (c. 1773), in Saunders, *Colonial Records*, IX:803-804.

CHAP. XXV.

An Act to amend sundry acts for the better regulating the pilotage in the several ports of this State.

WHEREAS great evil has arisen from slaves taking charge of vessels coming in or going out of the different ports of this State, without the master or owner being bound for their misconduct:

Be it therefore enacted by the General Assembly of the State of North-Carolina, and it is hereby enacted by the authority of the same, That from and after the first day of May next, the master or owner of any slave or slaves may apply to the Commissioners of Navigation, or a majority of them, in their respective ports, for a licence authorising such slave or slaves to pilot, and upon said Commissioners approving of his or their qualification, they shall grant such slave a branch or certificate in the name of his master or owner to pilot accordingly; whereupon said master or owner shall enter into bond with two good and sufficient securities in the sum of five hundred pounds, current money, for the faithful discharge of the duty of said slave: [. . .]

Laws of the State of North-Carolina, 1800, c. 25. The licensing of slaves as pilots was disallowed by law in 1812.

Slaves, understandably, worked reluctantly and required constant supervision to ensure the completion of tasks and to prevent escape. Laboring in the fields and forests, many suffered under the oversight of overseers. Competent overseers were exceptionally difficult to find. James Murray, in the Lower Cape Fear, complained that he had realized only half the production of indigo that he might have expected from his plantation, perhaps because his overseer had been too lenient. On the other hand, Penelope Dawson's overly harsh overseer aroused resentment to the point of rebellion among her slaves. Planter Charles Pettigrew in Washington County, severely critical of overseers, eventually decided to manage his plantation personally, if possible.

[. . .] [Edenton, December 1783]. We lived at a regular tavern, where the legal charge *per* day for 3 persons and 3 horses was 5 Spanish dollars (12 fl. Rhenish), and for four long days we had nothing but old geese, suckling pigs, and raw salad, there being no vinegar to be had in the whole place. Here was much a-do about nothing; half a dozen negroes were running about the house all day, and nothing was attended to, unless one saw to it himself. [. . .]

Schoepf, *Travels in the Confederation*, II:118.

[. . .] [1759]. "I have made about 1000 lb to my share this year, besides Rice and Tar and might have made clear double that quantity had my Overseer been good."

Tiffany, *Letters of James Murray*, 78n.

Dear Cousin,

I was very much surprised this morning on my first going out att meeting two of the negroes from Mr. Galland, Old Jack and the boy that was down last year, they complain most bitterly of hard treatment, they say they work very hard and are willing to continue so to do and live upon dry bread could they ever please the overseer, but that he beats them just as much without a fault as with one, Jacks says he had near killd him with the hoe on saturday as he was standing att his work and promised to give him a hundred lashes on monday, on which he left the place and has been ever since getting here, I would not have troubled you about it, but they are not willing to go back [. . .]

Pene Dawson

Eden House July 17th 1772

Penelope Dawson to Samuel Johnston, July 17, 1772, Hayes Papers, Southern Historical Collection.

Charles Pettigrew to Rebecca Tunstall

Washington [County] 22d. June 1803 [. . .]

We hoped to have seen you before this, but find it very difficult to find a time, in which we can with propriety leave home so long. We have no Overseer, choosing rather to oversee the negroes, than an Overseer & them too, without which Employers generally go to leeward. The negroes at the Lake plantation have commonly done better by themselves with a little direction than with such overseers as we have had. [. . .]

Sarah McCulloh Lemmon, ed., *The Pettigrew Papers*, 2 vols. to date (Raleigh: Division of Archives and History, Department of Cultural Resources, 1971-), I:307.

Slaves and masters ultimately reached a point of accommodation, a balance between expectations and demands. In the southern colonies and states, fieldwork on larger agricultural units often proceeded according either to the gang or the task system. Tobacco, grown more in the northern and western counties, ~~required~~ constant attention and hence lent itself to the gang ~~system, as was the case in Virginia.~~ Tasking may have characterized rice production in the Lower Cape Fear, as in South Carolina, and the tending of "turpentine forests" in the southeastern region of North Carolina. While Scotus Americanus implied the use of tasking, Janet Schaw indicated that the slaves she observed worked in gangs.

[. . .] Their work is performed by a daily task, allotted by their master or overseer, which they have generally done by one or two o'clock in the afternoon, and have the rest of the day for themselves, [. . .]

Scotus Americanus, "Informations Concerning the Province of North Carolina," 616.

On our arrival here the stalks of last year's crop still remained on the ground. At this I was greatly surprised, as the season was now so far advanced, I expected to have found the fields completely ploughed at least, if not sown and harrowed; but how much was my amazement increased to find that every instrument of husbandry was unknown here; not only all the various ploughs, but all the machinery used with such success at home, and that the only instrument used is a hoe, with which they at once till and plant the corn. To accomplish this a number of Negroes follow each other's tail the day long, and have a task assigned them, and it will take twenty at least to do as much work as two horses with a man and a boy would perform. [. . .]

Janet Schaw, *Journal of a Lady of Quality; Being the Narrative of a Journey from Scotland to the West Indies, North Carolina, and Portugal, in the Years 1774 and 1775*, ed. Evangeline W. Andrews and Charles M. Andrews (New Haven: Yale University Press, 1921), 163.

———

Brickell, Scotus Americanus, and Schaw noted that slaves were allowed to cultivate their own garden plots, raise poultry and hogs, and gather salable plants, like snakeroot, after finishing their assigned tasks. Such spare-time activities contributed to the

development of an internal, domestic economy among bondsmen that not only enabled them to supplement their meager food and clothing allowances, but also to accumulate property. Fearing that the latitude accorded slaves in pursuing their private economic fortunes might lead to competition for whites, as well as offer greater incentive to theft, North Carolina lawmakers first forbade slaves to keep livestock and later to grow tobacco in the principal tobacco-producing counties of the colony.

[. . .] they are allowed to plant a sufficient quantity of *Tobacco* [for] their own use, a part of which they sell, and likewise on *Sundays*, they gather *Snake-Root*, otherwise it would be excessive dear if the *Christians* were to gather it; with this and *Tobacco* they buy Hats, and other Necessaries for themselves, as *Linnen, Bracelets, Ribbons*, and several other Toys for their Wives and Mistresses.

John Brickell, *The Natural History of North Carolina*, (1737; reprint, Murfreesboro, N.C.: Johnson Publishing Co., 1968), 275.

[. . .] which they spend in working in their own private fields, consisting of 5 or 6 acres of ground, allowed them by their masters, for planting of rice, corn, potatoes, tobacco, &c. for their own use and profit, of which the industrious among them make a great deal. In some plantations, they have also the liberty to raise hogs and poultry, which, with the former articles, they are to dispose of to none but their masters (this is done to prevent bad consequences) for which, in exchange, when they do not chuse money, their masters give Osnaburgs, negro cloths, caps, hats, handkerchiefs, pipes, and knives. They do not plant in their fields for subsistence, but for [26] amusement, pleasure, and profit, their masters giving them clothes, and sufficient provisions from their granaries. [. . .]

Scotus Americanus, "Informations Concerning the Province of North Carolina," 616.

[. . .] The allowance for a Negro is a quart of Indian corn pr day, and a little piece of land which they cultivate much better than their Master. There they rear hogs and poultry, sow calabashes, etc. and are better provided for in every thing than the poorer white people with us. [. . .]

Schaw, *Journal of a Lady of Quality*, 176-177.

CHAPTER XXIV.

An Act Concerning Servants and Slaves. [. . .]

XLIV. And be it further Enacted, by the Authority aforesaid, That no slave shall be permited, on any Pretence whatsoever, to raise any Horses, Cattle or Hogs; and all Horses, Cattle and Hogs that Six Months from the Date thereof, shall belong to any Slave, or of any Slave's Mark in this Government, shall be seized and sold by the Church Wardens of the Parish where such Horses, Cattle or Hogs shall be, and the Profit thereof be applied, One Half to the Use of the said Parish, and the other Half to the Informer.

Laws of North Carolina, 1741, in Walter Clark, ed., *The State Records of North Carolina*, 16 vols. (11-26) (Raleigh: State of North Carolina, 1895-1906), XXIII:191, 201.

CHAPTER IV.

An Act to Amend the Staple of Tobacco, and prevent Frauds in his Majesty's Customs. [. . .]

IX. And be it further enacted by the authority aforesaid, that no slave within the Counties of Halifax, Northampton, Bute, Granville, Orange, Chatham, Edgecombe and Wake for his own benefit shall cultivate any Tobacco under the penalty of five pounds Proclamation Money, to be recovered from the Master, Owner or Overseer of such slave, by action of Debt before any jurisdiction having cognizance thereof, one-half to the informer and the other half to the use of the County where such slave shall reside.

Laws, 1774, in Clark, *State Records*, XXIII:948, 952.

Although the institution of slavery mandated bondage in perpetuity, not all slaves remained fixed in that condition. Some ran away, a subject that will be treated later; others obtained their freedom by manumission. The General Assembly in 1715 permitted masters to emancipate bondsmen, but it required freed slaves to leave the colony. The legislature altered that approach to liberation in 1741, allowing manumissions only for "meritorious services" as adjudged by the county courts. However, freed

bondsmen, if they wished, might remain in North Carolina. The slave owner had to post bond to guarantee that the freed slave would not become a burden to the public. Slave owners still might free their bondsmen without the approval of county courts, but such freed men had to leave the colony within six months and, once departed, could not return for longer than a month. Otherwise they risked being re-enslaved. In 1796 the General Assembly declared, as it had in 1777, that only the county courts could free slaves.

CHAPTER XLVI.

An Act Concerning Servants & Slaves. [. . .]

XVIII. And be it Further Enacted by the Authority aforesaid that no person within this Government shall make any contract with his or their Negro or Negroes for his or their freedom or Liberty that are Runaways or Refractory Negroes. Provided that this Act shall not hinder any man from setting his Negro free as a Reward for his, or their honest & Faithful service. And Provided that such Negro depart the Government within Six Months after his Freedom But if any Negro set free as aforesaid shall not within the time Limitted & according to the true Intent & Meaning of this Act depart the Government then such Negro or Negroes shall by the precinct Court be sold for Five Years to such person or persons as shall give security for their Transportation & the Moneys arising by such sale shall be paid into the Public Treasury.

Laws, 1715, in Clark, *State Records*, XXIII:62, 65.

CHAPTER XXIV.

An Act Concerning Servants and Slaves. [. . .]

LVI. And be it further Enacted, by the Authority aforesaid, That no Negro or Mulatto Slaves shall be set free, upon any Pretence whatsoever, except for meritorious Services, to be adjudged and allowed of by the County Court, and Licence thereupon first had and obtained; [. . .]

Laws, 1741, in Clark, *State Records*, XXIII:191, 203.

CHAP. V.

An Act to *amend, strengthen and confirm the several acts of Assembly of this State, against the emancipation of Slaves.*

WHEREAS doubts have arisen in the construction of the said acts, as to the extent of the liberation powers vested in the county courts, by an act passed in the year one thousand seven hundred and seventy-seven, chapter sixth, entitled "An act to prevent domestic insurrection," and another act passed in the year one thousand seven hundred and forty one, chapter twenty-nine:

I. *Be it therefore enacted by the General Assembly of the State of North-Carolina, and it is hereby enacted by the authority of the Same,* That no slave shall be set free in any case, or under any pretence whatever, except for meritorious services, to be adjudged of and allowed by the county court, and licence first had and obtained therefor; and that such liberation when entered of record, shall vest in the said slave, so as aforesaid liberated, all the right and privilege of a free born negro, any thing in the said act to the contrary notwithstanding.

Laws, 1796, c. 5.

State of North Carolina New Hanover County. Court of Pleas and quarter Sessions, June Term 1797

Know all men by these Presents that We John McLellan, George Hooper, Henry Urquhart and John Allan all of the County aforesaid, are held and firmly bound unto his Excellency Samuel Ashe esqr. Governor, Captain-General and Commander in Chief in and over the State aforesaid in the just and full sum of One thosuand Pounds, for the which payment will and truly to be made to his Excellency the Governor aforesaid his successors or assigns. We do hereby, jointly and severally, firmly by these present, bind our [selves] and each of us our Heirs Executors and Administrators, Sealed with our Souls and dated as above.

The Condition of the above Obligation is such, that Whereas, the 4 Justices presiding in the Court aforesaid at the Term aforesaid have on the Petition of the aforesaid John McLellan, emancipated and sett free, as fully and amply, as by the Laws of this State they are enabled, a certain female Negroe Slave, belonging to the said John McLellan named Maria and her four children named William Elizabeth, Margaret and Mary; Now in case the said female Negroe Slave Maria and her four Children William, Elizabeth, Margaret and Mary or either of them shall not in any manner whatsoever become chargeable to or in this or any other County within this State, then the above Obligation to be void otherwise to remain in full force and Virtue.

John McLellan (Seal), G. Hooper (Seal),
Henry Urquhart (Seal), John Allan (Seal)

Signed Sealed and Delivered
in presence of
James W. Walker

Bond, New Hanover County Court, June 1797, New Hanover County, Miscellaneous Records, Records of Slaves and Free Persons of Color, Emancipation Records, State Archives, Office of Archives and History, Raleigh.

After the Revolution, the General Assembly supplemented the county courts as an agency to liberate slaves. Although slave owners continued to use the county courts as evidenced by the manumissions of Joe and his son Alfred in Chowan County, they often bypassed the local jurisdictions to appeal directly to the legislature. Executors of estates particularly found the General Assembly useful as they sought to fulfill the wishes of the deceased as indicated by will or by oral or written instruction. At the same time, the legislature as well as the county courts emancipated slaves whose military service in the Revolution had aided the cause of independence.

On Motion of Mr. Iredell, It appearing to this Court that a Negro Man named Joe formerly the property of William Churton of this County Gentleman, but Set free by the last Will and Testament of the said William Churton, which the sanction and approbation of this Court at their Session in the month of March in the year one Thousand Seven hundred and sixty eight, at which time the said Negroe man Joe was adjudged a free Man Accordingly, has since that time rendered very Meritorious Services to Joseph Hewes and Robert Smith late of the said County Merchants; and that the said Joseph Hewes and Robert Smith, in Consideration of the same, did in the Month of May one thousand seven hundred and seventy seven Convey to the said Joe a negroe Boy Slave named Alfred (a son of the said negroe Man Joe by a negroe Woman named Rachel formerly the Property of George Blair of Edenton Merchant [Deceased] without receiving in fee any Pecuniary Consideration with the Express view and design that the said negroe Man Joe might hereof if the Said negroe boy shewed himself deserving of it Cause him to be made free and the said negroe boy having since that time as is represented to this Court, approved himself very dutifull and Obedient, to his said Father and rendered him meritorious Services which in the Opinion of his said Father well entitle him to Such Indulgence and the Said negroe Man Joe being therefore Willing to Set free the said negroe Boy, in Consequence of the benevolent intentions of his former Masters and his own meritorious Services, and Signifying in person his desire of and Consent to the same. It is therefore ordered and adjudged that the Said negroe boy Alfred be Set free accordingly, and that he be hareafter entitled to all the rights and priviledges of a free <*man*> Person [. . .]

> Minutes of the Chowan County Court of Pleas and Quarter Sessions, June 1782, State Archives, Office of Archives and History, Raleigh.

CHAPTER XLVIII.

An Act to emancipate Caesar, formerly a Servant of Samuel Yeargan, Deceased.

Whereas by the last will and testament of Samuel Yeargan, deceased, late of the county of Warren, he did desire in his said will that a certain negro man of his property, should after the death of his daughter Anne Alston, wife to William Alston, of Chatham county, be set free, for and during the full-term of fifty-five years: And whereas the said Anne being now dead, it is thought just and right the said last will and testament should be adhered to:

I. Be it therefore enacted by the General Assembly, That from and after the passing of this Act, that the aforesaid Caesar shall and may be at his own liberty, for and during the term mentioned in his master's will, upon the same footing, and under the same restrictions as other free negroes are intitled to in this State, and shall be known and called by the name of Caesar Henry; any law to the contrary notwithstanding. (Passed Jan. 6, 1787.)

Laws, 1787, in Clark, *State Records*, XXIV:850.

CHAPTER XVIII.

An Act to Emancipate a certain Negro Slave named Phillis, late the Property of George Jacobs, of the town of Wilmington, Deceased.

Whereas it is represented to the General Assembly that the aforesaid George Jacobs, deceased, in his last illness, did earnestly request that his n[e]gro slave named Phillis should be liberated for her great attention to her said master during her continuance with him, and more especially for her care and assiduity in his last illness: In order therefore to carry into effect the dying request of the said George Jacobs, deceased:

I. Be it Enacted by the General Assembly of the State of North Carolina, and it is hereby Enacted by the authority of the same, That from and after the passing of this Act, the aforesaid negro woman named Phillis, shall be emancipated and forever discharged from her bondage, in as full and ample manner as if she had been born free; any law, usage or custom to the contrary notwithstanding: And the said negro woman shall forever hereafter be known by the name of Phillis Freeman.

Laws, 1788, in Clark, *State Records*, XXIV:963.

CHAPTER LXX.

An Act for Enfranchising Ned Griffin, Late the Property of William Kitchen.

I. Whereas, Ned Griffin, late the property of William Kitchen, of Edgecomb county, was promised the full enjoyments of his liberty, on condition that he, the said Ned Griffin, should faithfully serve as a soldier in the continental line of this State for and during the term of twelve months; and whereas the said Ned Griffin did faithfully on his part perform the condition, and whereas it is just and reasonable that the said Ned Griffin should receive the reward promised for the services which he performed;

II. Be it therefore Enacted by the General Assembly of the State of North Carolina, and it is hereby Enacted by the authority of the same, That the said Ned Griffin, late the property of William Kitchen, shall forever hereafter be in every respect declared to be a freeman; and he shall be, and he is hereby enfranchised and forever delivered and discharged from the yoke of slavery; any law, usage or custom to the contrary thereof in anywise notwithstanding.

Laws, 1784, in Clark, *State Records*, XXIV:639.

To the Worshipfull the Justices of Perqs. County Court now Siting The Petition of the Subscribers in Behalf of a Certain Negro Man Named James formerly the Property of Thomas Newby of the County Aforesaid Humbly Sheweth

That some time in the year 1776 the said Thomas Newby Manumited the said Negro man James, That since that the Greater part of his time he has been Employed as a Seaman, and has made Several Voyages from this State and Virginia in the time of the Last War, and that he has Twice, or more been made Prisoner by the British. That he Embraced the Earliest oppertunity in Making his Escape to Return to this Country being the place of his Nativity, where he has a Wife and Children That Once during the War between America and Great Britain he Entered himself onboard of one of the American Armed Vessels. That during the Time of his Servitude with his said Master, he behaved himself as a faithfull Servant, and Rendered his Master great Services as a Seaman, and that since his freedom we have reasons to Believe he has Continued to behave Orderly and Honest. We are therefore willing to hope that on your Worships Maturely considering and Weighing every particular, you will bee of opinion that the Poor fellow is Intitled to some small share of Merrit, If that should be your worships Opinion. We earnestly Solicit (in the poor fellows behalf) that you Will permit an Entry to be made on the Minutes of Your Court allowing the Fellow to have done Something Meritorious and for that Reason you will give a Sanction to his freedom, that he may with safety Visit his Wife and Children, when It will be in his power to Render further Services to this State, as an able Seaman, and your petitioners Shall ever pray etc.

Thos. Newby, Thomas Harvey,
Robt. Devows, Pete Lawton, M.
Newbould, Thomas Sutton, Geoe.
Whidlew, John Craicy, Caleb
Winslow, Samuel McClanahan.

[*Endorsed*:]
A Petition on behalf
of Negro James
Granted

Petition for emancipation, undated, Perquimans County, Miscellaneous Records, Slave Records, Petitions for Emancipation, State Archives, Office of Archives and History, Raleigh.

The onset of the Revolution reinforced a longstanding antipathy toward slavery among many Quakers and heightened their determination to renounce the institution. As a result of pronouncements of the Yearly Meeting of the Society of Friends of North Carolina, between 1774 and 1776, Quakers began to liberate their bondsmen. In 1777 the General Assembly, observing that Quakers had not posted bond to ensure the proper conduct of the freed slaves, declared the manumissions illegal and empowered county sheriffs to apprehend and sell at auction the recently liberated slaves. The following year, the legislature confirmed the sales, though bondsmen like Job in Perquimans County found freedom irresistible. After the legislature rebuffed an attempt by the Quakers to repeal the statutes of 1777 and 1778, the Friends resorted to legal channels, the county courts, to free their slaves; but all the while, implicitly or explicitly, they expressed their opposition to bondage.

CHAPTER VI.

An Act to prevent domestic Insurrections, and for other Purposes.

I. Whereas the evil and pernicious Practice of freeing Slaves in this State, ought at this alarming and critical Time to be guarded against by every friend and Wellwisher to his Country:

II. Be it therefore enacted by the General Assembly of the State of North Carolina, and by the Authority of the same, That no Negro or Mulatto Slave shall hereafter be set free, except for meritorious Services, to be adjudged of and allowed by the County Court, and Licence first had and obtained thereupon. And when any Slave is or shall be set free by his or her Master or Owner otherwise than is herein before directed, it shall and may be lawful for any Free holder in this State, to apprehend and take up such Slave, and deliver him or her to the Sheriff of the County, who, on receiving such Slave, shall give such Freeholder a Receipt for the same; and the Sheriff shall commit all such Slaves to the Gaol of the County, there to remain until the next Court to be held for such County; and the Court of the County shall order all such confined slaves to be sold during the Term to the highest Bidder.

Laws, 1777, in Clark, *State Records*, XXIV:14-15.

Some Quakers in North Carolina have lately emancipated their Negroes, & the Assembly have passed a Law for apprehending the Negroes, and selling them as Slaves; the Money to be put into the public Treasury. The Reason assigned for this Proceeding, I am told, is that the Quakers refuse to give Security that the Negroes shall not become Burthensome to the State. I think this Conduct cannot be vindicated; it is infamous & a violent breach of Faith, as well as an intrusion upon private Property, & directly repugnant to every principle upon which we contend for Liberty. It certainly would have been better to allow of the Emancipation & passed a Law that such Negroes as could not maintain themselves, & actually became burthensome to the State, should, when they became so, be hired as Servants to some Person who should maintain them. [. . .]

Hugh Buckner Johnston, ed., "The Journal of Ebenezer Hazard in North Carolina, 1777 and 1778," *North Carolina Historical Review* 36 (July 1959): 362-363.

The Public on account of Negroes Sold by Order of Court by Richard Skinner Sheriff October 1788.

Dr.

1788 Oct 17 To Committing and releasing

13 Negroes @ 5/4   £3   9 4

  To Notiseing the former Owners   1 14 8

To Summoning 21 Witnesses	2 16
To Paid for finding John Moore Esqr.	19 7 6
Paid the States atty. his fee for late of 12.	24
Paid for Guarding the Gaol	7 4
Commission for Selling £763.14. @ 2/ 8d	19 10
Paid freeholders for apprehend'g negroes	137 2 6
	£215 4 0

due the Public Ballance this Amount which is in
Bonds, the Sale being on Credit   548 10

£763 14 0

Cr

1788 October 17th By Amount of Sales of Negroes
Sold by Order of Court of this date   £763 14 0
Errors Excepted July 13th. 1789,

Dr. Richd. Skinner Sheriff

[*Endorsed*:]
Richard Skinners Account
for Sale of Negroes
Octr. 17th 1788

Sale of Slaves by Richard Skinner, October 1788, Perquimans County, Miscellaneous Records, Slave Records, Miscellaneous Slave Papers, State Archives, Office of Archives and History, Raleigh.

December 15, 1796

TEN DOLLARS REWARD.

MADE his escape, on the 16th instant, near Hertford, in Perquimans, my negro fellow JOB; he is about 5 feet 6 inches, rather black, has remarkable small feet and hands, 25 or 30 years of age; he was bred in Perquimans, and probably he may be lurking about there, as he has a mother and other relations not far from Hertford; he was one of the negroes emancipated by the Quakers, and taken up and sold by order of court; it is more than probable that they may wish to secret him; all those who offend that way, may rely on being dealt with in the utmost severity of the law. The above reward will be given to any person that will deliver said negro to me, or confine him in gaol so that I get him again, together with all reasonable expences.

THOMAS POOL.

Pasquotank, Nov. 28, 1796

Advertisement, *North Carolina Gazette* (New Bern), in Parker, *Stealing a Little Freedom*, 31.

Mr. [Abner] Nash, from the Committee appointed to take under consideration the Petition of the people of Pasquotank, relative to the Slaves liberated by the Quakers, Reported as follows:

Your Committee having taken under consideration the Petition of the People of Pasquotank, relative to the Slaves liberated by the Quakers, came to the following opinion, that the Conduct of the said Quakers in setting their Slaves free, at a time when our open and declared Enemies were endeavoring to bring about an Insurrection of the Slaves, was highly criminal and reprehensible, and that it was also directly contrary to the known and Established Laws of the Country. [. . .]

House Journal, January 26, 1779, in Clark, *State Records*, XIII:659-660.

To the County Court now about to Sit in Perquimans.

The Petition of the Several Subscribers Humbly Sheweth

That whereas Samuel Smith a few Years Ago Manumitted a Servant Man Named Peter (Whose Mother was an Indian and Father a Negroe) which Said Servant Man hath not been taken up nor Sold by the Court; And as he hath hither to Always been an Orderly Servant and never that we know of been Accused of any Villany, But on the Contrary Hath done Several Meritorious Actions in Destroying Vermin Such as Bears Wolves wild Cats and Foxes Therefore we pray that the Court may take it into Consideration and Order and Adjuge that he may remain Free and unmolested as long as he behaves himself well And your Petitioners the Several Subscribers, as in Duty Bound shall ever pray [. . .]

Petition for Emancipation, April 6, 1782, Perquimans County, Miscellaneous Records, Slave Records, Petitions for Emancipation, State Archives.

Family

Their lives disrupted and their culture threatened upon their transportation to the New World, African Americans stubbornly resisted the changes forced upon them, adhering as much as possible to the traditions of their homeland. Maintaining Africanisms in their new environment under the constant pressure of bondage proved daunting, but slaves often retained their names and controlled the naming of their children. Such autonomy did not significantly challenge the hegemony of their masters. African names often reflected unique personal circumstances or possessed considerable social significance. Parents commonly named children after the day of the week on which they were born or according to their birth order in the family. Hence, among Frederick Gregg's slaves were Quashey (Sunday), Cuffee (Friday), and Samboe (second son among the Hausa). While some names survived intact, many were compromised, perhaps by an abbreviation or approximation of a name—Joe for Cudgo (Monday), or by the mispronunciation or Anglicization of African-sounding names—Venus for Cubena (Tuesday). Classical names may have been alterations of African derivatives reflecting personal characteristics—Herculus in Gregg's household from *heke*, the Mende noun meaning a large, wild animal.

No. 3 Letter C continued

A List of Negroe Slaves belonging to Frederick Gregg.

Left at Cape Fear North Carolina in August 1773.

No.	Men Names	Trade or Employment	No.	Women and Girls Names	Employment.
1	Manuel	Taylor	42	Venus	Cook
2	Glascoe	Shoemaker	43	Lucinda	
3	Quecie	Cooper	44	Dianah	Cooke
4	Ben	Ditto	45	Phoebe	Washer woman

5	Jonathan D	Ditto	46	Long Phoebe	
6	Ambrose	Ditto	47	Sapho	
7	Berwick	Ditto	48	Sophia	
8	Samboe	Ditto	49	Bess	
9	Sampson	Miller	50	Manetta	
10	Quashey D.		51	Bessey	
11	Joe		52	Cloe D.	
12	Sam		53	Hannah	
13	New Joe		54	Jenny	
14	John	Coachman	55	Bella	
15	Frank	Sailor	56	Peggy	House Wench
16	Doctor Frank		57	Her Daughter	
17	French Manuel		58	Bennabee	
18	Hector	Sailor	59	Old Lucy	
19	Jack Chambers		60	Little Venus	
20	Derry		61	Ester	
21	Little Tom		62	Charlotte	
22	Antrim D.	Baker			
23	Isaac				
24	Arthur				
25	Old Cuffy				
26	Young Cuffy				
27	Little Cuffy				
28	Dick	Fisherman			
29	Hereford	Tanner			
30	Simon				
31	Mercury				
32	Appier				
33	Hurricane	Sailor			

34	Scotland	
35	Bedford	
36	Same	
37	Tom	
38	Ned	Sailor
39	Herculus	
40	Charles	
41	Little Charles	

Those marked D. are Dead Since Memorialist left Carolina.

Loyalist Claim of Frederick Gregg, in Audit Office 13/119, British Records, State Archives, Office of Archives and History, Raleigh.

Under adversity, slaves sought to form a household or family unit, an institution of the greatest benefit for bondsmen, for it provided emotional satisfaction and the means for perpetuating African culture. Emanuel and his wife Frank, listed in a 1695 inventory of former governor Seth Sothel, constituted one of the earliest slave families in North Carolina. Legislation in 1729 recognized the occurrence of slave marriages, though the practice was left to the discretion of slave owners. As described by John Brickell, bondsmen solemnized marriages in ritualistic ceremonies, rites that might have seemed fanciful to whites, but possessed deeper meaning for blacks. Although slave unions lacked positive legal support, and were subject to dissolution at the discretion of masters who might sell or otherwise alienate bondsmen, the owners had a vested interest in maintaining the family unit. Marriage and the family may have helped slaves cope with their lot in life, or at least make them less likely to run away, as evidenced by the plea of Callum to Penelope Dawson.

No Carolina

In Obedience to an Order of the Right Honoble Lds proprietors Deputies we whose names are hereunder written being mett att the house of Seth Sothrell Esqr Deseased att Salmon Creeke have upon Oath appraised the sd Seth Sothrells Estate as it was prsented to us by Mr John Hawkins att the Sd place vizt

One Negro Man named Emanuel Frank his Wife [. . .]

Inventory of Seth Sothel, July 9, 1695, in J. Bryan Grimes, comp., *North Carolina Wills and Inventories* (Raleigh: Edwards & Broughton Printing Co., 1912), 560.

CHAPTER V.

An additional Act to an Act, for appointing Toll-Books, and for preventing People from driving Horses, Cattle, or Hogs, to other Persons' Lands. [. . .]

IX. Provided always, That nothing in this Act shall be construed to prevent any Persons from sending his Slaves on his lawful Business, with a pass, in Writing; nor to hinder Neighbours' Negroes intermarrying together, so that Licence being first had and obtained of their several Masters.

Laws of North Carolina, 1729, in Walter Clark, ed., *The State Records of North Carolina*, 16 vols. (11-26) (Raleigh: State of North Carolina, 1895-1906), XXIII:112, 114.

Their *Marriages* are generally performed amongst themselves, there being very little ceremony used upon that Head; for the Man makes the Woman a Present, such as a *Brass Ring* or some other Toy, which if she accepts of, becomes his Wife; but if ever they part from each other, which frequently happens, upon any little Disgust, she returns his Present: These kind of Contracts no longer binding them, than the Woman keeps the Pledge given her. [. . .]

John Brickell, *The Natural History of North Carolina* (1737; reprint, Murfreesboro, N.C.: Johnson Publishing Co., 1968), 274.

[. . .] I am afraid Callum will plague you a little he would not rest till I promisd to let you know that one of the girls that are hired out is his wife, and entreats very hard that she may be sufferd to stay on the plantation I never met with such a pleader, I told him I did not imagine it would be to any purpose to trouble you about it but he insisted upon it that if you knew she was his wife you would let her stay, as it would prevent his ever running about from the plantation so that he seems to think himself a person of the utmost consequence. [. . .]

Penelope Dawson to Samuel Johnston, December 17, 1774, Hayes Papers, Southern Historical Collection, Manuscripts Department, Wilson Library, University of North Carolina at Chapel Hill.

African Americans clung tenaciously to their family ties. A mother on the auction block begged pitifully, but in vain, that she and her daughter not be separated. Advertisements and notices of runaways often indicated that they intended to join spouses or other family members. Slaves also resorted to their knowledge of plants and poisons to protect loved ones. Upon learning that his daughter might be purchased by Josiah Nash, whose wife mistreated the slaves, Sambo apparently concocted some poison or touck (juice of the manioc root, or tuckahoe) and solicited Nash's slaves to administer the substance to Mrs. Nash.

[March 1778]. Whilst at Wilmington, I witnessed a heart-rending spectacle, the sale of a negro family under the sheriff's hammer. They were driven in from the country, like swine for market. A poor wench clung to a little daughter, and implored, with the most agonizing supplication, that they might not be separated. But alas, either the master or circumstances were inexorable — they were sold to different purchasers. The husband and residue of the family were knocked off to the highest bidder. [. . .]

Winslow C. Watson, ed., *Men and Times of the Revolution; or, Memoirs of Elkanah Watson* (New York: Dana and Co., 1856), 58.

March 30, 1793

TWENTY DOLLARS REWARD,

WILL be given, for taking up and delivering to me, or securing so that I get him again, a NEGRO MAN, named ISAAC, who ran away about fifteen days past. He is about five feet nine inches high, well made and twenty five years of age. He took with him a short blue coat and breeches, and I have reasons to believe that he is lurking in Perquimans county, where I understand he has lately taken a wife. [. . .]

Advertisement, *State Gazette of North Carolina* (Edenton), in Freddie L. Parker, ed., *Stealing a Little Freedom: Advertisements for Slave Runaways in North Carolina, 1791-1840* (New York: Garland Publishing Co., 1994), 22.

Micaj. Thomas to Thomas Blount

31st. August 1783

Dear Sir

The negro wench I purchased of you is Run away and I have reason to beleave that She Is gon back to washington. I Shall esteem it as the greatest favour If you will instruct the bearer Mr. Collings how to proseed so as to catch her, and bid my reasonable Reward to any of your neighbours that will take her up and Send her to your Self. I will pay any expense to any man that you would contract with to bring her to me. If She can not be taken while this man is down, I am expect She will indevour to git back to where She was Raised, but am convinced that She will call for her Husband With Respect I am Dear Sr. your most Obedient Humble Servant

MICAJ. THOMAS [. . .]

Alice Barnwell Keith, ed., *The John Gray Blount Papers*, Vol. 1, *1764-1789* (Raleigh: Division of Archives and History, Department of Cultural Resources, 1952), 99.

Pasquotank County. Att a Special Court Begun Opined and held at the Court house on Relfes point on the Seventh day of August 1761 To try a Negro fellow called Sambo the property of Edward Williams for several crimes whereof he stands Charged as preparing Poison for Mrs. Mary Nash the wife of Josiah Nash Esqr. and [induising] Endeavouring to have the same given to her and as Accessary to the Adminnestering thereof. [. . .]

Then Came a Negro Wench of Mr. Nash called Tamer and being Examined says that David told her he could destroy all the House by some touck that the Prisoner could give him and that he had given some of the same to his Mistress. [. . .]

Then the aforesaid David being called says that the Prisoner told him that his Master should not have the Negro Girl he wanted to Buy (meaning the prisoners daughter) by reason his Mistress was bad to the Negros and that he (the prisoner) would give him some Touck to give his Mistress that Would make her Sick and if it didnot do come to him and he would give him some more that would do. [. . .]

Trial of Sambo, August 1761, Minutes of the Pasquotank County Court of Pleas and Quarter Sessions, State Archives, Office of Archives and History, Raleigh. The court found Sambo guilty and sentenced him to be castrated. Sambo survived the sentence. William L. Saunders, ed., *The Colonial Records of North Carolina*, 10 vols. (Raleigh: State of North Carolina, 1886-1890), VI:740.

As the trial of Sambo indicated, slaves continually harkened to their African culture to organize and understand their lives. To counter the enormous power of white society, they turned to traditional African specialists in medicine and religiosity: conjurers, obeah men, or medicine men, such as Sambo. Bristoe, in Johnston County, prepared concoctions that would affect the lives of blacks and whites alike. By means of potions, Will, in Dobbs County, reputedly brought Sarah Wiggens under his control, fathered a child by her, and claimed that he could similarly seduce other women in the county.

State of North Carolina Johnston County. At a Court Called at the Court House of said County for the Purpose of Trying sundry negroes for the Crimes hereafter mentioned. 16th October 1779 Present <*The Worshipfull*> Needham Bryan, James Lockhart, John Sanders, Richard Warren, Kedar Powell, <*Esquires*> William Bryan, John Vinson, Benjamin Crufford, Joseph Ingram <*Gentlemen freeholders etc.*>

<*Negro Bristoe belonging to Col. Sml Smith Senr.*> The Dendant appeared at the Bar and Charged and Examined, denied the Charge.

<*Jacob evidence vs. Bristoe belonging to N Farmer*> that Bristoe dug a hole and put Brandy in it and rubed Toms foot with it and cut a piece of root and gave it to Lucy to prevent her going to Drowning Creek, that Bristoe was to give him something to make his master Sell him, for which he Jacob was to give five [*torn*] and half a [*illegible*] but he never went. That he once rubed dust in his hand to prevent his master from whiping him.

<*Hannah. belonging to Mrs. Durham*> Evidence that Jacob told her that he got some kind of Stuff from Bristoe to make his master Sell him, and also gave her something which he got from Bristoe to give her mistress and Billy Durham, to make them better to the negroes; and that she gave her mistress some four times.

<*Jane evidence belonging to Cap Lee*> That Capt Williams Ceaser told her that he gave her milk to prevent her having children.

<*Tom evidence belonging to G Allen*> That he made a hole in the ground and put Brandy into it and rubed his right ancle with the mud. and gave him a piece of root to chew in order to make his master Buy his wife, that Bristoe told him he had been doing business for Dempsters Negroes to make them be returned home again.

The Court taking the same under consideration Ordered that the said Bristoe be taken to the public Whiping post and receive 30 Lashes.

> Nm. Bryan, Jas. Lockhart, John Sanders,
> Richd. Warren, Kedar Powell, Joseph Ingram.
> W. Bryan, Benjn. Crafford, John Vinson

Trial of sundry Negroes, October 16, 1779, Johnston County, Miscellaneous Records, Special Court for the Trial of Negroes, State Archives, Office of Archives and History, Raleigh.

The Deposition and Examination of Sarah Wiggins, the Wife of Gershom Wiggins taken at Dobbs County the 12th day of April 1772.

That about three Years ago Will a Negroe Fellow belonging to her father Benjn. Herring came to her House and asking several Questions about one Gibbs and Curtis and some others pulled out a Bottle with some rum in it and asked her to drink of it she refused several times to drink of it but was at last prevailed on Drink of it, that after she had drank of it she found her self strangely sick, and asked him what kind of rum it was he had he Answered it was not for any but his friends. That some time after he came with another Bottle and got her to drink of it under a pretence of Giving her of that she had drank of it before and it had an odd taste which enduced her to Ask him what was in it He answered her it was Herbs that it had such an Effect on her that it Caused her head be as tho she was drunk and took away her Senses. he asked whether any Person had used her ill and said that if they had he Could make them love her better than ever they did. That she veryly at different times he gave her some Liquid thing to drink which always deprived her of her Senses and by that means had Carnal knowledge of her Body, That after he had begot the first Child on her Body he threatned that if any Person would or did talk about it he would say or do something that would hurt them and She understood that he would poison them because he said had seen poeple poison one another and that he Could poison others himself, that she verily believes he knows how to poison anyone, and that She was afraid that if She disobliged him he would poison her, [. . .] And that he told her he had a good Will to go and try Laney Wiggins for he could lye with the best of the Women if he tryed them and that they talked of that was nothing for he could go to her Sister Darcus and serve her As he had her this deponent. That the said Will afterwards told her that he had Carnal Knowledge of her which he Afterwards denied, and said he would have done it if she had not desired her not.

<div align="right">Sarah <<em>her mark</em>> Wiggens</div>

The Deposition and Examination of Sarah Wiggens, April 12, 1772, New Bern District Superior Court, Criminal Action Papers, State Archives, Office of Archives and History, Raleigh.

The fragments of evidence concerning the condition of slaves in North Carolina reveal a pattern of life that differed little from that of bondsmen in other southern colonies and states. However, some observers believed North Carolinians accorded their bondsmen better treatment than did South Carolinians and Virginians. Smaller agricultural units and smaller average slave-holdings may have contributed to less demanding work and more personal concern for slaves.

The slaves in North Carolina are fewer in number, better clothed and better fed, than in South, and are of consequence better servants.

Mark A. De Wolfe Howe, ed., "Journal of Josiah Quincy, Junior, 1773," *Proceedings of the Massachusetts Historical Society* 49 (June 1916): 463.

[. . .] Good usage is what alone can make the negroes well attached to their masters interest. The inhabitants of Carolina, sensible of this, treat these valuable servants in an indulgent manner, and something like rational beings. [. . .]

Scotus Americanus, "Informations Concerning the Province of North Carolina, Etc." (1773), in *Some North Carolina Tracts of the Eighteenth Century*, ed. William K. Boyd, *North Carolina Historical Review* 3 (October 1926): 616.

Nonetheless, the lot of the slave was not an enviable one. The maintenance of Africans little burdened their masters. The wearing apparel distributed to slaves was scant; for children it was often nonexistent. Their diet was as meager as their clothing, unless they belonged to owners who permitted them to tend garden plots. Otherwise, they subsisted on corn products and an occasional allowance of meat. The fare may well have been worse on plantations supervised by overseers for absentee landowners, as evidenced by the complaint of Penelope Dawson's slaves. While the bondsmen of Thomas Blount received a little consideration, one of the Reverend John Urmston's slaves perished for want of care.

The *Children* of both Sexes wear little or no Cloaths, except in the *Winter*, and many of the young Men and Women work stark naked in the Plantations in the hot Season, except a piece of Cloath (out of decency) to cover their Nakedness; upon which Account they are not very expensive to the Planters for their Cloathing. [. . .]

Brickell, *Natural History of North Carolina*, 276.

[. . .] [October 17, 1745]. I would just observe that all that part of North Carolina that we came through is a poor flat Sandy soil & scarce any thing grows on it but Pines & a long course Grass in many places, on which their Cattle feed, but one meets now & then with what they call Savannah's, very little better than the rest, only that it bears much more Grass & is better Range.

The People, especially those that live most Southerly are very indolent & lazy & keep Negroes to do their work, which they half starve, allowing ym no more in general than a half peck of Indian Corn a week & a pint of Salt, & no Cloaths but a Breech Clout.

"William Logan's Journal of a Journey to Georgia, 1745," *Pennsylvania Magazine of History and Biography* 36 (1912): 15.

[. . .] The keep of a negro here does not come to a great figure, since the daily ration is but a quart of maize, and rarely a little meat or salted fish. Only those negroes kept for house-service are better cared for. Well-disposed masters clothe their negroes once a year, and give them a suit of coarse woollen cloth, two rough shirts, and a pair of shoes. But they who have the largest droves keep them the worst, let them run naked mostly or in rags, and accustom them as much as possible to hunger, but exact of them steady work. [. . .]

Johann David Schoepf, *Travels in the Confederation, 1783-1784*, 2 vols., trans. and ed. Alfred J. Morrison (Philadelphia: W. J. Campbell, 1911), II:147.

I have sent a day sooner than Intended on account of the boy that brings this who came to me yesterday morning with a grevious complaint of being starved, and that he was sure the Negroes would all leave the plantation if there was not an alteration made, [. . .]

Penelope Dawson to Samuel Johnston, July 6, 1770, Hayes Papers, Southern Historical Collection.

Thomas Blount to John Gray Blount

27th Nov. 1783

Dear Sir, [. . .]

[3] Thursday night 27th Nov. 1783

I declined sending the negroes down today because of the coldness & wetness of the weather Jerry & Miles being but thinly clad. but they will start by daylight To-morrow morning. [. . .]

Keith, *Blount Papers*, I:133-134.

[. . .] we are all naked and the winter very severe; I've lost a Negroe this winter, he has merely starved for want of cloths and a warm lodging, and I shall be forced to sell the other Negroe, to keep us till I can hear from you, which I pray may be with all speed. [. . .]

Rev. John Urmston to Secretary, SPG, February 14, 1715/6, in Robert J. Cain, ed., *The Church of England in North Carolina: Documents, 1699-1741*, Volume X of *The Colonial Records of North Carolina* [*Second Series*], ed. Mattie Erma Edwards Parker, William S. Price Jr., and Robert J. Cain (Raleigh: Division of Archives and History, Department of Cultural Resources [projected multivolume series, 1963-], 1999), 212.

Despite the constraints imposed upon their lives, slaves found or made time for leisure activities. Owners traditionally gave their bondsmen the day off on Sunday; masters might at any time grant their slaves a "holiday," as traveler Johann David Schoepf discovered to his dismay at the Edenton ferry. Blacks joined the crowds at horse races, betting small amounts, while young male slaves rode the mounts. At home, they enjoyed dancing and games. From their plantations, slaves "rambled" many miles at night to "entertainments" or dances at neighboring plantations, though gatherings at houses for drinking and dancing were forbidden by law in 1794. Still, as long as slaves appeared for work the following morning, there was little that masters could do about their nocturnal travels.

[Edenton, June 15, 1777]. Hot, sultry Weather, but the Heat a little alleviated by a Breeze from the Sound. This being Sunday, the Negroes have an Holy-Day, according to the Custom of the Southern States. [. . .]

Hugh Buckner Johnston, ed., "The Journal of Ebenezer Hazard in North Carolina, 1777 and 1778," *North Carolina Historical Review* 36 (July 1959): 364.

Full four days we stayed at Edenton waiting to be set over Albemarle Sound: the trouble was not wind and weather, but the scurvy negligence of the man who by permission of a high authority keeps the ferry. He had allowed the negroes to go across the Sound with the boat for a holiday, not at all solicitous about travellers who might arrive in the mean time. No people can be so greedy after holidays as the whites and blacks here, and none with less reason, for at no time do they work so as to need a long rest. It is difficult to say which are the best creatures, the whites here or their blacks, or which have been formed by the others; but in either case the example is bad. The white men are all the time complaining that the blacks will not work, and they themselves do nothing. The white men complain further that they cannot trust the faithless blacks, and they set them a dubious model. [. . .]

Schoepf, *Travels in the Confederation*, II:117-118.

[New Bern, Saturday, November 24, 1787]. I have attended the Races yesterday and today rather from motives of curiosity than any love to this Amusement, and think I shall hardly be prevailed on to go ten Steps in future to see any Horse Race—The objections and inconveniences attending this kind of Amusement, obvious to me, are, [. . .]

By wagering and betting; much quarreling wrangling, Anger, Swearing & drinking is created and takes place, I saw it on the present occasion prevalent from the highest to the lowest — I saw white Boys, and Negroes eagerly betting 1/ 2/ a quart of Rum, a drink of Grog &c, as well as Gentlemen betting high — [. . .]

Many accidents happen on these occasions —

One of the Riders a Negroe boy, who rid one of the Horses yesterday, was, while at full speed thrown from his Horse, by a Cow being in the Road and the Horse driving against her in the hurry of the Race — The poor Lad was badly hurt in the Head and bled much — [. . .]

[December 25, 1787]. After Breakfasting I returned to Tarborough. I dined with Andrew Grier. After dinner saw a dance of Negroes to the Banjo in his Yard.

Lida Tunstall Rodman, ed., *Journal of a Tour to North Carolina by William Attmore* (Chapel Hill: James Sprunt Historical Publications, 1922), 17-18, 43.

But instead of retiring to rest, as might naturally be concluded he would be glad to do, he generally sets out from home, and walks six or seven miles in the night, be the weather ever so sultry, to a negroe dance, in which he performs with astonishing agility, and the most vigorous exertions, keeping time and cadence, most exactly, with the music of a banjor (a large hollow instrument with three strings), and a quaqua (somewhat resembling a drum), until he exhausts himself, and scarcely has time, or strength, to return home before the hour he is called forth to toil next morning.

John F. D. Smyth, *A Tour of the United States of America*, 2 vols. (1784; reprint, New York: Arno Press, 1968), I:46.

CHAP. IV.

An Act *to prevent the owners of slaves from hiring to them their time, to make compensation to Patrolls, and to restrain the abuses committed by free negroes and mulattoes* [. . .]

And be it further enacted, That no person shall grant permission for any meeting or meetings of the negroes of others, or people of colour, at his, her or their houses, or on his, her or their plantation, for the purpose of drinking or dancing, under the penalty of forfeiting ten pounds on conviction of such offence in any court having jurisdiction thereof, unless such slave shall have a special permit in writing or otherwise from his or her owner for that purpose.

Laws of the State of North-Carolina, 1794, c. 4.

Religion constituted a powerful tool by which Africans preserved and transmitted their culture, coped with their bondage, and resisted their subordination to white society. The continuing influx of blacks during the eighteenth century reinforced African religiosity; most bondsmen in North Carolina carried on their indigenous faiths, grounded in a holistic approach to life that led them to believe that humans could control their immediate circumstances as well as their future condition. When Janet Schaw attended the funeral of a white, slaves appeared, and she witnessed the song, dance, and celebratory behavior that Africans often exhibited at their own burials, designed to assuage the pain of bereavement and ensure an appropriate continuing link between the living and the deceased.

They were no sooner gone than the Negroes assembled to perform their part of the funeral rites, which they did by running, jumping, crying and various exercises. They are a noble troop, the best in all the country; [. . .]

Janet Schaw, *Journal of a Lady of Quality; Being the Narrative of a Journey from Scotland to the West Indies, North Carolina, and Portugal, in Years 1774 and 1775,* ed. Evangeline W. Andrews and Charles M. Andrews (New Haven: Yale University Press, 1921), 171.

Missionaries of the Church of England, recognized as the official church in North Carolina as early as 1669 by the Fundamental Constitutions, made an earnest effort during the eighteenth century to convert Africans to Christianity. But adherence to traditional forms of worship, linguistic differences between blacks and whites, the opposition of slave owners who thought conversion bestowed freedom upon the bondsmen (despite the

disclaimer found in the Fundamental Constitutions), and other factors undermined their effectiveness. But the clerics persevered. They informed the secretary of the Society for the Propagation of the Gospel, the religious agency in England that sent most missionaries to North Carolina, of the number of blacks and whites that they baptized. Still, the Reverend James Reed in New Bern was careful in his approach to baptism and pessimistic about the success of the church in converting slaves.

98. Since Charity obliges us to wish well to the Souls of all men, and Religion ought to alter nothing in any man's civil Estate or Right, It shall be lawful for Slaves, as all others, to enter them selves and be of what church any of them shall think best, and thereof be as fully members as any freeman. But yet, no Slave shall hereby be exempted from that civil dominion his Master has over him, but be in all other things in the same State and condition he was in before.

Fundamental Constitutions, 1669, in Mattie Erma Edwards Parker, ed., *North Carolina Charters and Constitutions, 1578-1698*, Volume I of *The Colonial Records of North Carolina* [*Second Series*], ed. Mattie Erma Edwards Parker, William S. Price Jr., and Robert J. Cain (Raleigh: Division of Archives and History, Department of Cultural Resources [projected multivolume series, 1963-], 1963), 150.

<212> Mr. [Ebenezer] Taylor to the Secretary [to the S.P.G., Rev. David Humphreys.]

Perquimons Precinct Apl. 23d 1719

Honoured Sir [. . .]

These two Persons were Esqr. DuckenFields Slaves (The Gentleman with whom I liv'd most of this Year, and whose House was our Church all this Year) This Gentleman had severall other Slaves, who were as Sensible and Civil, and as much Inclined to Christianity and things that are Good: as ever I knew any Slaves in any place, wherever I have been <220> and indeed soe are the Slaves generally in this Province, and many of the Slaves of this Countrey, I am perswaded would be Converted Baptiz'd and Sav'd if their Masters were not so wicked as they are, and did not oppose their Conversion, Baptism and Salvation so much as they doe. I had for sometime great hopes of being the Minister that should convert and Baptize the rest of Esqr. Duckenfilds Slaves, which I was very desirous and Ambitious to be, and I would have begrudg'd no pains, but would most freely and with the greatest Pleasure have done all I could to Promote and Accomplish this so great and so good a work, And in Order thereunto I was preparing 4 more of them for Baptisme, and had taught one of those 4 their Catechism very perfectly and the other 3 a good part of it, and now as I was about this good Work, the Enemies to the Conversion and Baptism of Slaves, industriously and very busily buzz'd into the Peoples Ears, that all Slaves that were Baptiz'd were to be set free, and this silly Buckbear so greatly Scar'd Esqr. DuckenField, That he told me plainly I should Baptize no more of his Slaves till the Society had got a Law made in England that no Baptiz'd Slave, should be set free because he is Baptiz'd and send it here, and many more are of the same mind, and soe this good Work <221> was knock'd in the head, which is a great Trouble to me, because so many Slaves are so very desirous to become Christians without any Expectation of being set free when they are Baptiz'd. I fear this good Work will not be reviv'd and prosper here till such a Law is Enacted by the Parliament of Great Britain, and this people are acquainted with it, For I perceive nothing else will satisfie them.

Cain, *Church of England in North Carolina*, X:258, 261.

Mr. [Alexander] Stewart to the Secretary [to the S.P.G., Rev. Daniel Burton.]

GLEBE NEAR BATH N. CAROLINA Nov 6 1763

Revd SIR:

As soon as my health would permit, I set out for the benefit of the sea air, to a part of Hyde County called Atamuskeet (this Place I formerly informed the society) is separated by an impassable morass from the other parts of that country and is only to be come at by water and upwards of 70 miles from Bath, while I was there I preached twice at the Chapel and baptized 64 white children one Adult white, 11 black adults and 11 do. infants, and at the other chapels in Hyde County 42 white infants and 5 black do. [. . .]

Saunders, *Colonial Records*, VI:995.

J. Reed to the Secretary [to the S.P.G., Rev. Daniel Burton.]

NEWBERN June 26 1760.

REVd SIR [. . .]

We have no Indians amongst us, but the greatest part of the negroes in the whole county, may too justly be accounted heathens 'tis impossible for ministers in such extensive counties, to instruct them in the principles of the Christian religion & their masters will not take the least pains to do it themselves. I baptize all those whose masters become sureties for them, but never baptize any negro infants or Children upon any other terms. [. . .]

Saunders, *Colonial Records*, VI:264-265.

Among other denominations with an interest in the religious life of slaves, the Baptists and Methodists made the greatest impact. By the time of the Revolution the Society of Friends, or Quakers, had decided to liberate their bondsmen, and the Moravians accepted, on a partially nondiscriminatory basis, those blacks who showed a willingness to join their church. Yet it was the evangelical fervor unleashed by the Great Awakening, and the renunciation of slavery by the Reverend George Whitefield who spearheaded the movement, that betokened the greatest promise for slaves. The Baptists, with their democratic, inclusive, nonliturgical approach to religion, made the most immediate appeal to slaves. After the Revolution the Methodists, led by Francis Asbury, took the lead in opposing slavery, often at great risk to themselves, and incorporating Africans into the membership of the church.

Nov. 13. Our Negro, Johann Samuel, whose baptism was the first sacramental act in the consecration of our Saal three years ago was today present as a candidate for the Communion.

Salem Diary, 1774, in Adelaide L. Fries et al., eds., *Records of the Moravians in North Carolina*, 12 vols. to date (Raleigh: North Carolina Historical Commission, 1922-), II:821.

Mr. [John] Barnett to the Secretary [to the S.P.G., Rev. Daniel Burton.]

BRUNSWICK Cape Fear Feby 3rd 1766

REVEREND SIR, [. . .]

New light baptists are very numerous in the southern parts of this parish — The most illiterate among them are their Teachers even Negroes speak in their Meetings — They lately sent to me to offer the use of their meeting house where I propose to officiate once in two months.

Saunders, *Colonial Records*, VII:163-164.

[February 12, 1803]. [. . .] at the town (Wilmington), another ferry, and another storm in crossing made our journey for the day unpleasant enough: we arrived, however, at our own house in proper time. We found the church ceiled, and the dwelling improved. I met the people of colour, leaders and stewards; we have eight hundred and seventy-eight Africans, and a few whites in fellowship. [. . .]

Grady L. Carroll, ed., *Francis Asbury in North Carolina: The North Carolina Portions of the Journal of Francis Asbury* (Nashville, Tenn.: Parthenon Press, 1964), 204.

———————

Illiteracy handicapped attempts by churches and their itinerant agents to convert slaves. But whites, many of whom were also illiterate, saw little reason to educate their own children, much less the slaves: literacy would allow bondsmen to forge passes with which to trade goods and travel illegally, promote communication among themselves, and engender the possibility of conspiracy and revolt. Still, as Brickell observed and as advertisements for runaway slaves testified, some bondsmen were literate.

There are several *Blacks* born here that can Read and Write, others that are bred to Trades, and prove good Artists in many of them. [. . .]

Brickell, *Natural History of North Carolina*, 275.

RAN away from the Subscribers, on *Roanoke* River, a Negro Fellow, named *Thomas Boman*, a very good Black-Smith, near six Feet high, has a little Blemish in one of his Eyes, good Sett of Teeth, well made sensible Fellow; and slow of Speech; he can read, write, and cypher; [. . .]

Robert West, sen.
Robert West, jun.

N.B. *Tis supposed he is gone towards* South-Carolina, *as he was seen over* Tar River.

North Carolina Gazette (New Bern), March 13, 1752.

132. October 10, 1796

RAN away from the subscriber, about 5 miles from Moore court house, N. Carolina, on Thursday night, the 15th inst. two Negroes, a man and woman, the man about 30 years of age, very black, sensible, speaks good English, reads and writes tolerable well, strong and well made, very active, especially in running and jumping, has a scar on one of his legs, occasioned by the cut of an axe, is about 5 feet 6 inches high [. . .]

Advertisement, *North Carolina Journal* (Halifax), in Parker, *Stealing a Little Freedom*, 54.

A few slaves may have received the rudiments of education from clergymen, particularly Anglican ministers, in North Carolina. Under the auspices of Dr. Bray's Associates, a philanthropic branch of the Church of England dedicated to the education of slaves in America, the Anglican clergy attempted to establish schools in Edenton, Bath, Wilmington, and elsewhere. Although such efforts often were undermined by geography, poverty, and prejudice among other factors, the Reverend John Barnett briefly but successfully operated two schools for blacks in Northampton County.

Rev. Daniel Earl to Rev. John Waring

No. Carolina Edenton
3 October 1761

Sir

Mr. Hazlewood Merchant in this Town shewed me a Letter from you, wherein you signified to him, that a Society called Dr. Bray's Associates were desirous that a School may be opened here for the

Education of Negroe Children; under the Care of him, Mr. Child, and myself; [. . .] I have used my utmost Endeavours to recommend their beneficient and charitable Design to the Inhabitants of this Town; and to Represent it in that Light that it ought to Appear to all who Profess our Holy Religion. [. . .] They all Allow of the great Expediency of the Design, but say, that as their Circumstances are low and Depressed, (which is generally the Case) they can't spare their Negroes from their Service at the Age that they are susceptible of Erudition: And those that are in Affluent Circumstances are so very few, that the Number of Children sent by them would be so inconsiderable, as not be worth any Person's Acceptance; [. . .]

John C. Van Horne, ed., *Religious Philanthropy and Colonial Slavery: The American Correspondence of the Associates of Dr. Bray, 1717-1777* (Urbana: University of Illinois Press, 1985), 164-165. Rev. Waring was the secretary to Dr. Bray's Associates.

Rev. Alexander Stewart to Rev. John Waring

Bath N: Carolina August the 12th. 1762

Revd. Sir,

Your Favour of the 20th. of April, Came safe to hand a few days ago, and I shou'd be unworthy of the Honour the Associates have done me in appointing me Superintendent of their Seminary here; Did I not, to the utmost of my Capacity & Station endeavour to promote this their truly pious & Christian Design. To this purpose I have already made known the Associates Intentions at the Church In Bath & the Several Chappels within my Parish, & with pleasure found most People approvers & many that promised to be encouragers of this publick Utility. But, there are many Difficulties which we Labour under in this Province, which other Provinces are Exempt from. For the towns of N: Carolina are all of them very Small, & Bath particularly has the fewest Inhabitants of any of them; so that the Number of Schollars to fill up a School cou'd by no means be had in any of the towns of this Province. Our towns likewise on the Seaboard, (where Negroes are most to be had,) are all of them built on very wide Rivers, often Impracticable to Cross; this Cutts off one half of the Country Children & added to the Expence of boarding Negroe Children, the Loss of their time, & the Prejudices of the Ignorant, are the Difficulties which at present Stand in the Way. [. . .]

Van Horne, *Religious Philanthropy and Colonial Slavery*, 176.

Lewis De Rosset to Rev. John Waring

[Wilmington, North Carolina, 22 April 1765]

Revd. Sir,

I am to acknowledge the Rect. of your Esteemed favour which together with the Box of books you sent came to my hands last Year. I should have Answered your Letter before now, but I thought it would be best to deferr writing untill I had tryed all Methods to carry into Execution the Laudable Designs of the Society, But am very sorry to say that all my endeavours for that purpose have proved Innefectual as I can find no Person here properly qualified to Instruct the black Children in the manner you propose. And If such a one could be found yet in this Country Twenty Pounds Sterling is by far too little to Support them and Am much afraid that nothing more can be got here, for I have spoke to several Gentlemen here who I thought might send black children to School and proposed to them to give the Master or Mistress something out of their own pocketts to encourage the undertaking, but have not found them willing to doe that. I thought that the same Master or Mistress might teach white Children as well as black their Parents paying for it, but there seems in this a repugnancy in them to have their children instructed with their Slaves, which though in my Opinion a very trifling reason, yet their prejudices are very deeply Rooted.

Van Horne, *Religious Philanthropy and Colonial Slavery*, 226.

Rev. John Barnett to Rev. John Waring

[Northampton, North Carolina, 9 June 1770]

Revd. Sir

I reciev'd your favor of March 1769 in February last, which informs me of the Box of Books being sent to Cape Fear for the use of the Negroes.

I being distant thence upwards of two hundred miles, and hardly any Communication thence to this part of the Province; have given directions to a Friend there to distribute them among those Negroes who can read a little; always giving the preference to those who formerly composed part of my Black Congregations.

In September last I inform'd the Associates of the endeavors I was using to establish two Negroe Schools in these parts and of the prospects of Success I had.

About Sixty Adult Slaves have Joyfully accepted the offer of Instruction; and to the honor of their Owners let me add, they are willing to Indulge them with opportunities for learning to read on Sundays and all Evenings.

For Six months past, I have employed two men to teach in different parts of my Neighborhood and the good progress many of the Negroes have made sufficiently evidences *their* diligence and the *teachers* faithfulness.

I last winter purchased of a Merchant here about three dozen Spelling and some other Books proper for the use of the Negroes, who with a view of furthering the Charitable design let me have them at something about prime Cost.

Van Horne, *Religious Philanthropy and Colonial Slavery*, 291.

The Slave Code

The earliest extant legislation in North Carolina that fully addressed slavery, limited bondage to nonwhites and defined slaves as chattel, dates from 1715, part of a revisal of the colony's laws at that time. However, the existence of slavery before 1715 elicited earlier statutes that dealt with the bonded population, allusions to which can be found in the public records as seen below. The statute of 1715, replaced by a lengthier law in 1741 and accompanied by numerous minor enactments during the eighteenth century, established a body of legislation that constituted the "slave code" for North Carolina.

North Carolina Ss. To the Honorable the Generall Court

Mr. Frederick Jones is Plaintiff against Samuel Payne Defendant in A Plea of the Case and Setteth forth that whereas by an Act of Assembly made in the yeare of our Lord God One Thousand Six Hundred Nynety and Nyne itt is Enacted that whosoever Shall Entertain or privately harbour any Runaways either white Servants or Negroes above One Night Shall for every Twenty four Houres afterwards pay Tenn Shillings to the Master of the Said Servant either white Servant or Negro and if the Master Shall Susteyine any Dammage above the Said Servants labour for the time of Such Concealment he Shall have his remedy att Law for Such Dammage over and above the Penalty hereby provided [. . .]

General Court, March 1704, in William S. Price Jr., ed., *North Carolina Higher-Court Records, 1702-1708*, Volume IV of *The Colonial Records of North Carolina [Second Series]*, ed. Mattie Erma Edwards Parker, William S. Price Jr., and Robert J. Cain (Raleigh: Division of Archives and History, Department of Cultural Resources [projected multivolume series, 1963-], 1974), 94.

Thos. Pendleton by Danl. Richardson his attorney Comes to prosecute his Information against Daniell Guthrie and Saith that Whereas In and by an act Made by The Grand assembly of this province between the 2th Day of Janry. anno Domini 1705/6 and the Eight Day of March then next following Intitled an act Consearneing Servants and Slaves by which Said act it was (inter alia) Enacted in the following or the like words (videlicet) and be it further Enacted by the authority aforesaid That whosoever buy Sell Trade or Trucke Borrow or lend to or with any Servant or Servants Slave or Slaves without the

Lycence or Consent of his or their master or owner for any Comodity whatsoever Shall forfeite and pay for every Such offence Ten pounds to be recovered as aforesaid as in and by the Said act [. . .]

General Court, 1714, in William S. Price Jr., ed., *North Carolina Higher-Court Minutes, 1709-1723*, Volume V of *The Colonial Records of North Carolina [Second Series]*, ed. Mattie Erma Edwards Parker, William S. Price Jr., and Robert J. Cain (Raleigh: Division of Archives and History, Department of Cultural Resources [projected multivolume series, 1963-], 1974), 68.

<24> Upon reading this Day the Bill of Complaint of James Tooke Merchant against Miles Cary therein Setting Forth that whereas one Danll. Akehurst Esqr. by his Last Will and Testament bearing date the 11th Xber. 1698 did and bequeath unto his Daughter Filia Christi among other Legacies therein Expressed all his concerns in Carolina by Form and Vertue of which Bequest and the will aforesaid one Jo. Jordan by an intermarriage with the Said Fillia Christi the only Daughter and heyr of the Said Daniell became Lawfully Seized and possessed of all and Singular the goods and Chattles and other Estate of the Said Daniell in Carolina and particularly of one negro Slave called Stephen which the Said Joseph held and enjoyed for the Space of twelve years and further that he the Said Tooke purchased the Said Slave of the Said Joseph and being in a Lawfull possession thereof by the Lawfull Sale and delivery in Markett overt of the Said Joseph, one Miles Cary of Virginia by Collusion pretending a right or title from one Anne Akehurst widow in Virginia to the Said Slave altho the Said Joseph had been possessed thereof for the Space of Twelve years as aforesaid Commenced an Action of Trespass against the form of a Statute made by the Grand Assembly of this Province Intituled an Act Concerning Servants and Slaves against him the Said Tooke in the Generall Court of this Province [. . .]

Court of Chancery, April 1714, in Price, *North Carolina Higher-Court Minutes, 1709-1723*, V:481.

———

The slave code placed bonded Africans totally under the control of their owners, limited any discretionary autonomy of blacks, and restricted interaction between slaves and whites. In addition to proscribing slave resistance in any form and providing a means

for dealing with slave criminality, topics that will be addressed separately, the code prohibited slaves from traveling without written permission from their owners. Eventually, the use of forged passes by sympathetic whites or by literate slaves evoked legislation that mandated corporal punishment for slaves bearing bogus passes.

CHAPTER XLVI.

An Act Concerning Servants & Slaves. [. . .]

VIII. And Be it Further Enacted by the Authority afors'd that no Master nor Mistress Nor Overseer shall give leave to any Negro, Mulatto or Indyan Slave (except such as wait upon their persons or wear Liverys) to go out of their Plantations without a Ticket or White servant along with them which Ticket at least the name of either the Master, Mistress, or Overseer shall be subscribed & therein shall be incerted the place from whence he came & whither going under the Penalty of Five Shillings besides the charge of paying for the taking up of such slave or runaway.

Laws of North Carolina, 1715, in Walter Clark, ed., *The State Records of North Carolina*, 16 vols. (11-26) (Raleigh: State of North Carolina, 1895-1906), XXIII:62-63.

Granville County ss. Phillemon Hawkins Esqr. Complains to me one of his majesties Justices of the peace for the said County that he has just Cause to Support that James Martin Son of Rachel Martin has forged a pass with the hand of James paine and Joshua Hortons Esqrs., therto for a negro man Slave to him Belonging Calld Bob that is now Obsconded and Runaway.

I therfore Command you in his majesties name to take the Body of the said James and Cause him to Apeare before me or Some other Justice of the peace for the said County to Answear the above Complaint also make Due the turn how you have Executed this warrent Given under my hand this 26th Day of July 1762.

Will. Johnson Jp

To Zach: Bullock
To Execute and Return

Writ, July 26, 1762, Granville County, Miscellaneous Records, Civil Actions Concerning Slaves and Free Persons of Color, State Archives, Office of Archives and History, Raleigh.

CHAP. IV.

An *Act* to amend an Act, entitled, *An Act to prevent Thefts and Robberies by Slaves, free Negroes and Mulattoes*, passed at Tarborough in the Year one thousand seven hundred and eighty-seven; [. . .]

II. And whereas it is also represented to this General Assembly, that numbers of slaves, belonging to citizens of this state, pass from county to county, and to other states, and when apprehended produce a free pass or certificate signed with the name of some citizen of the place where they are owned, which [*torn*] represented are often forged, and frequently even by some other servant or slave, an [*torn*] there is no law now in force in this state to prevent such pernicious practices: *Be it f[urthe]r enacted by the authority aforesaid,* That from and after the passing of this act, if any slave shall be guilty of producing such forged free pass or certificate, he or she so offending, shall on conviction, suffer such corporal punishment as a court shall inflict (death excepted) to be tried in the same manner as slaves are tried for other capital offences.

Laws of the State of North-Carolina, 1791, c. 4.

The slave code also prohibited blacks from hunting with weapons and dogs except on the plantations of their owners. In those instances, slave owners had to obtain the permission of the county court to arm the slaves and post a bond for their proper behavior. Illicit outings by club-wielding slaves created alarm among whites in Wake County.

CHAPTER XXIV.

An Act Concerning Servants and Slaves. [. . .]

[1741] XL. And be it further Enacted, by the Authority aforesaid, That no Slave shall go armed with Gun, Sword, Club or other Weapon, or shall keep any such Weapon, or shall Hunt or Range in the Woods, upon any pretence whatsoever (except such Slave or Slaves who shall have a Certificate, [. . .]

XLI. Provided always, That nothing in this Act shall be construed or extended, to prohibit or debar any Master or Owner of any Slave or Slaves within this Government from employing any one Slave in each and every district Plantation, from hunting in the Woods on their Master's Lands with a Gun, to preserve his or her Stock, or to kill Game for his or her Family.

XLII. Provided Also, That such Master or Owner shall first deliver into the County Court an Account in Writing of the name of any such Slave to be employed as aforesaid, and the Chairman of the Court shall sign a Certificate that such Slave is allowed to carry a Gun, and hunt in the woods on his Master's or Mistress Lands: And the Master, Mistress or Overseer of such Slave shall give him the said Certificate, which such Slave shall always carry about him, on Pain of being apprehended and punished as aforesaid: Anything hereinbefore contained to the contrary notwithstanding. [. . .]

CHAPTER VI.

An additional Act to an Act concerning servants and slaves. [. . .]

[1753] VIII. And be it Enacted by the authority aforesaid, That no Slave shall hunt or range in the Woods with a Dog or Dogs, except such as shall have a Certificate for hunting, obtained as is in this Act directed: And if any Slave shall be found offending herein, it shall and may be lawful for any Person or Persons to kill and destroy the said Dog or Dogs, and to bring the said Slave before the next Magistrate, who shall on due Proof of his Offence, order the said Slave such Correction as he shall judge reasonable, not exceeding Thirty Lashes.

Laws, 1741, 1753, in Clark, *State Records*, XXIII:191, 201, 388-389.

State of North Carolina.

Know all men by these Presents that we Benjamin Brown and Henderson Standin are held and firmly bound unto Charles Johnson Esqr. Chairman and the rest of the Justices of Chowan County Court in the Just and full Sum of two hundred and fifty Pounds to the which payment well and Truly to be made and done we Bind our Selves and Each of our heirs Executers and administraters Jointly and Severally firmly By these presents Sealed with our Seals and Dated this 15th Day of March 1798.

The Condition of the above obligation is Such that whereas the above Bounden Benjamin Brown hath obtained leave of this worshipfull court, for his Negroe man Merick to Carry a Gun on his Said Masters Land — He Shall well and Truly demean himself and do no Injury with his Said Gunn to any Person or persons whatever Then This obligation tobe Void or Else to remain in full force and virtue.

B. Brown (Seal)
Hendn. Standin (Seal)

Signed Sealed and Delivd.
in presence of
Norfleet

> Bond, March 15, 1798, Chowan County, Miscellaneous Records, Slave Records, State Archives, Office of Archives and History, Raleigh.

Ordered that whereas it hath lately been a practice of Sundry Slaves in this County Especially fishing upon Crabb Tree and Walnut Creeks to carry Clubbs loaded on the Ends with Lead or Pewter, Contrary to the Act of Assembly, to the Anoyance of the Inhabitants, which may be attended with Dangerous and evil Consequences, the Court therefore Appoint the Chairman to Cause to be put up Advertisements, at the Court House and other Public places in this County, Requiring the Masters Mistresses or Owners of Slaves, to prohibit their Slaves from Carrying Such unlawfull weapons, testifying them at the Same time that if they therein fail the Majistrates, will Strictly put in Execution the Law against Such an evil and Dangerous Practice.

> Minutes of the Wake County Court of Pleas and Quarter Sessions, September 1774, State Archives, Office of Archives and History, Raleigh.

The slave code regulated the behavior of whites as well as blacks. It required all whites to apprehend runaways and to serve as slave patrollers, subjects that will be addressed later. Whites were forbidden to "entertain" or "harbor" slaves belonging to others. Still, the prosecution of whites and the need to reiterate the ban

on harboring slaves at the end of the eighteenth century showed that whites ignored legal strictures when it suited their purposes.

CHAPTER XLVI.

An Act Concerning Servants & Slaves. [. . .]

VII. And Be It Further Enacted by the Authority afors'd that if any person or persons shall entertain or Harbour any Runaway Servant or Slave above one Night he or they so offending shall for every Four & Twenty hours afterwards forfeit & pay the sum of Tenn Shillings to the Master or Mistress of such Servant or Slave together with all Costs, Losses & damages which the Master or Mistress shall sustain by means of such entertainment or Concealment to be recovered in any Court of Record within this Government [. . .]

Laws, 1715, in Clark, *State Records*, XXIII:62-63.

On Complaint of Thomas Jenkins Complaining that Elinor Berry hath Entertained his neagro and on hearing of Evidence it is the Courts Opinion that the said Elinor Berry is Guilty whereupon it is Ordered she be in the Sherriffs Custody till she give Security to Comply with the act of assembly and pay the fees. [. . .]

Minutes of the Onslow County Court of Pleas and Quarter Sessions, July 1742, State Archives, Office of Archives and History, Raleigh.

State of North Carolina Onslow County.

To the Sheriff of the County of Onslow afforsaid (Greeting) We Command you that you take Body of John Hatch Gentlemen (if to be found in your Bailiwick) and him Safely keep so that you have him before the Justices of the Next Inferiour Court of pleas and Quarter Sessions, to be held for said County at the Court House on New River on the Second Monday in April <January> Next then and there to Answer Eli. West in a plea or for Consealing and harbouring a negro, etc. etc. Damage to him Said West five Hundred Thousand pounds our Currency.

Herein find not and have you then and there this Writ Witness Will Cray clerk afoursaid given at the Clerks Office the 9th of October since the 6th year of our Independancy Ano Domini 1781.

W. Cray jp

Delivered at the Sheriffs
House Decmbr. 16th 1781.

Writ, October 9, 1781, Onslow County, Miscellaneous Records, Slave (Civil Actions
Concerning), State Archives, Office of Archives and History, Raleigh.

CHAP. IV.

An *Act* to amend an Act, entitled, *An Act to prevent Thefts and Robberies
by Slaves, free Negroes and Mulattoes,* passed at Tarborough in the Year
one thousand seven hundred and eighty-seven; [. . .]

I. *Be it enacted by the General Assembly of the state of North-Carolina, and it is
hereby enacted by the authority of the same,* That from after the passing of this
act, it shall not be lawful for any merchant or trader within this state to
harbour or trade with any slave, free negro or mulatto in their store
houses, shops, or tenements wherein they keep goods and
merchandize, at any time between sun-set and sun-rise, or on the
Sabbath-day, without a pass from his, her or their master, mistress, or
overseer, or from some justice of the peace, expressing the time when
and the business for which they go. [. . .]

Laws, 1791, c. 4.

———

**As a corollary to entertaining slaves, the law forbade whites to
buy from, sell to, or trade with slaves unless the bondsmen had
written permission from their owners. However, the effort to
reduce competition for white merchants and diminish the
incentive for slaves to steal from their masters proved fruitless.
Advertisements, petitions to the legislature, and the usual,
ongoing legislation attested to the difficulty of enforcing laws
that tried to ban a practice beneficial both to slaves and to
unscrupulous whites.**

CHAPTER XLVI.

An Act Concerning Servants & Slaves. [. . .]

X. And Be It Further Enacted by the Authority afors'd that
whosoever shall buy, sell, Trade, Truck, Borrow or Lend to or with any
Servant or Servants or Slave or Slaves without the Licence or Consent in

Writing under the Hand of his or her or their Master or Owners for any Condition whatsoever such person or persons so offending contrary to the true Intent & Meaning of this Act shall forfeit treble the Value of the thing Bought, sold, Traded or Trucked or Borrowed or lent. [. . .]

Laws, 1715, in Clark, *State Records*, XXIII:62, 64.

Advertisements.

Clearmont, Sept. 21, 1764

THIS is to inform the Public, that as I have such repeated Acts of Villany committed on my Plantation, by my own Negroes, in stealing my Corn, Potatoes, &c. and carrying the same to Town, and there dispose of them to Persons who make it their constant Practice to deal with Negroes: I am, for the future, determined to prosecute, with the utmost Rigour of the Law, any Person or Persons that shall deal in any Manner or Respect whatsoever with any of my Negroes, without their first producing to the Purchaser a Certificate, signed by Me, of their having Leave to dispose of the Commodity offered for Sale. And any Person that will inform Me, so that his Testimony will support a legal Prosecution, of any Person or Persons hereafter dealing with any of my Slaves, without the Certificate aforesaid, shall be paid a Reward of *Forty-Shillings* Proclamation Money, for each Prosecution which his Evidence will support, by

Thomas Clifford Howe.

North Carolina Magazine; or, Universal Intelligencer (New Bern), September 21, 1764.

North Carolina Granville County
September 15th 1773

To the Honorable Mr. Speaker and Gentlemen of the General Assembly
Your Petitioners the Inhabitants of this County think it our Duty to inform you that we suffer considerably in our Properties by Illdisposed Persons dealing with our Slaves in a Clandestine Manner. We humbly apprehend that if a Law for that Purpose was enacted inflicting severe Penalties on the Violators thereof it might be attended with the desired Effect in putting a Stop to that pernicious Practise or we pray that some other Measure may be taken as your venerable Body shall think more

Suitable to discourage so growing an Evil. That the Lord may direct and assist you in all your Determinations so as they tend to promote his Glory and the Publick Good of this Province is the Prayers of

Samuel Smith, [. . .]

Petition from the Inhabitants of Granville County to the Speaker and Assembly, September 15, 1773, Petitions - no action taken, Lower House Papers, Session of March 1774, General Assembly Session Records, Colonial (Upper and Lower House), State Archives, Office of Archives and History, Raleigh.

CHAPTER VII.

An Act to amend the several Acts of Assembly to prevent dealing or Trafficking with Slaves.

Whereas the laws and regulations made to prevent dealing and trafficking with slaves, have been found insufficient to prevent that pernicious practice:

I. Be it therefore Enacted by the General Assembly of the State of North Carolina, and it is hereby Enacted by the authority of the same, That if any free person shall either buy from or sell to any slave or slaves, any kind of goods or commodities whatsoever, or any other thing, without a permission in writing, setting forth the identical article or articles such slave or slaves may have for sale from the master, mistress or other person having the management of such slave or slaves, every such free person shall on conviction forfeit and pay the sum of ten pounds, and be further liable to pay all damages that may accrue in consequence of such trading or trafficking; one half thereof to the person informing, the other half to the person injured, to be levied of his or her property as other recoveries by law; and if the offender shall not have sufficient property to satisfy the judgment, then such offender shall be committed to close custody, and shall remain in prison without bail or mainprize for any time not exceeding three months.

II. And be it further Enacted, That if any slave or slaves shall hereafter offer any article whatever for sale, without permission from his or her owner, master or overseer, it shall or may be lawful for any person knowing the same, to apprehend such slave or slaves, and on due proof of the offence being made on oath before a Justice of the Peace of the county, he may order the said slave or slaves to receive any number of lashes, not exceeding thirty-nine, on his, her or their bare back. Provided nevertheless, That this Act shall not have effect or be in force until after the first day of March next.

Laws, 1788, in Clark, *State Records*, XXIV:956.

The slave code also forbade whites to steal or entice slaves away from their owners, a capital offense in neighboring Virginia and South Carolina. Still, whites in North Carolina often proved willing to avail themselves of the human property of others. While surveying the Virginia-North Carolina boundary in 1728, William Byrd and his party found a black family that may have been surreptitiously settled on land owned by whites.

No. 822 AN ACT TO PREVENT THE INVEIGLING, STEALING AND CARRYING AWAY NEGROES AND OTHER SLAVES IN THIS PROVINCE; [. . .]

I. *And be it enacted* by his Excellency, James Glen, Esquire, Governor-in-chief and Captain General, in and over his Majesty's Province of South Carolina, by and with the advice and consent of his Majesty's council, and the House of Assembly of the said Province, and by the authority of the same, That from and immediately after the twenty-fourth day of June next, all and every person or persons, who shall inveigle, steal and carry away any negro or other slave or slaves, or shall hire, aid or counsel any person or persons to inveigle, steal or carry away, as aforesaid, any such slave, so as the owner or employer of such slave or slaves shall be deprived of the use and benefit of such slave or slaves, or that shall aid any such slave in running away or departing from his master's or employer's service shall be, and he, she and they is and are hereby declared to be, guilty of a felony; and being thereof convicted or attainted by verdict or confession or being indicted thereof shall stand mute, or will not directly answer [to] the indictment, or will peremptorily challenge above the number of twenty of the jury, shall suffer death as felons, and be excluded and debarred of the benefit of clergy.

Laws, 1754, in David J. McCord, ed., *The Statutes at Large of South Carolina*, 22 vols. ed. Thomas Cooper, David J. McCord, and successive secretaries of state (Columbia, S.C.: A. S. Johnston, 1836-1898), VII:426.

North Carolina Granville County ss. To all Sheriffs Headboroughs and Constables in his Majesty's Province of North Carolina to whom these Presents shall come.

Whereas Robert Washington and George Andrews of the County of Northampton in the Province aforesaid have this Day made Oath before me William Johnson Esq. one of his Majesty's Justices of the Peace for the aforesaid County of Granville that on Sunday last William Andrews of the said County of Northampton was robbed of a Negroe Man Slave named London to him belonging, and also a Negroe Woman named Phebe, and a Negroe Girl named Hannah the Property of a certain Mary Penny; and Thomas Murrell of a Negroe Man named Sam, by Henry Sharp John Sharp junior. Jacob Sharp Marcus Sharp George Underwood James Underwood and John Underwood, who have since fled for the same, and are not yet apprehended.

Therefore in his Majesty's name I charge and command you in your several Counties and Precincts to search diligently for the said Persons and to make Hue and Cry after them from Town to Town and from County to County as well by Horsemen as Footmen, and if you shall find the said Persons or either of them that then you apprehend and bring him or them before a Justice of the Peace of the County where he or they shall be taken to be dealt with as the Law directs. And further you are hereby respectively impowered and commanded to take and raise such Aid and Assistance within your several Districts as shall be sufficient for the effectual apprehending and securing the said Robbers. Given under my Hand and Seal this third Day of June in the Year of our Lord one thousand seven hundred and sixty two.

William Johnson (Seal)

Writ, June 3, 1762, Granville County, Miscellaneous Records, Miscellaneous Records of Slaves and Free Persons of Color, State Archives, Office of Archives and History, Raleigh.

Ordered that Dick a Negroe fellow the Property of Benjamin Payton Living Near Beauty hill in South Carolina be taken by the Sheriff out of the Custody of Charity Cruse, in order that he may be Delt with as the Law Direct, it appearing to this Court By the Oath of James Geavens that said Negroe is the Property of the said Benjamin and was stole from him by a certain Person Named Welch.

Minutes of the Cumberland County Court of Pleas and Quarter Sessions, August 1763, State Archives, Office of Archives and History, Raleigh.

[Currituck County, March 11, 1728]. We had encampt so early, that we found time in the Evening to walk near half a Mile into the Woods. There we came upon a Family of Mulattoes, that call'd themselves free, tho' by the Shyness of the Master of the House, who took care to keep least in Sight, their Freedom seem'd a little Doubtful. It is certain many Slaves Shelter themselves in this Obscure Part of the World, nor will any of their righteous Neighbours discover them. On the Contrary, they find their Account in Settling such Fugitives on some out-of-the-way-corner of their Land, to raise Stocks for a mean and inconsiderable Share, well knowing their Condition makes it necessary for them to Submit to any Terms.

William K. Boyd, ed., *William Byrd's Histories of the Dividing Line Betwixt Virginia and North Carolina* (Raleigh: North Carolina Historical Commission, 1929), 56.

The General Assembly also enjoined interracial sexual liaisons. The revisal of 1715 followed Virginia legislation of 1705 that not only prohibited marriages between blacks and whites but also forbade clergy and justices of the peace from performing such marital rites. Later statutes, beginning in 1723, apparently recognized the formal unions of blacks and whites when denominating as taxables (persons subject to a capitation or poll tax) whites who had married blacks and persons of "mixed blood." Nevertheless, the laws did not sanction legally the solemnization of interracial marriages as revealed by the prosecution of the Reverend John Blacknall.

CHAP. XLIX.

An act concerning Servants and Slaves. [. . .]

XIX. And for a further prevention of that abominable mixture and spurious issue, which hereafter may increase in this her majesty's colony and dominion, as well by English, and other white men and women intermarrying with negros or mulattoes, as by their unlawful coition with them, *Be it enacted, by the authority aforesaid, and it is hereby enacted,* That whatsoever English, or other white man or woman, being free, shall intermarry with a negro or mulatto man or woman, bond or free, shall, by judgment of the county court, be committed to prison, and there remain, during the space of six months, without bail or mainprize; and shall forfeit and pay ten pounds current money of Virginia, to the use of the parish, as aforesaid.

XX. *And be it further enacted,* That no minister of the church of England, or other minister, or person whatsoever, within this colony and dominion, shall hereafter wittingly presume to marry a white man with a negro or mulatto woman; or to marry a white woman with a negro or mulatto man, upon pain of forfeiting and paying, for every such marriage the sum of ten thousand pounds of tobacco; [. . .]

Laws, 1705, in William Waller Hening, ed., *The Statutes at Large; Being a Collection of All the Laws of Virginia*, 13 vols., 2d ed. (Philadelphia: the editor, by Thomas Desilver, 1820-1823), III:447, 453-454.

CHAPTER XLVI.

An Act Concerning Servants & Slaves. [. . .]

XVI. And Be It Further Enacted By the Authority aforesaid that no White man or woman shall intermarry with any Negro, Mulatto or Indyan Man or Woman under the penalty of Fifty Pounds for each White man or woman.

XVII. And Be It Further Enacted that no Clergyman, Justice of the Peace or other person licensed to marry shall hereafter presume to celebrate such marriage under the like Penalty of Fifty pounds for every such marriage [. . .]

Laws, 1715, in Clark, *State Records*, XXIII:62, 65.

CHAPTER V.

An Act for an additional Tax on all free Negroes, Mulattoes, Mustees, and such Persons, Male and Female, as now are, or hereafter shall be, intermarried with any such Persons, resident in this Government. [. . .]

III. And be it further Enacted, by the Authority aforesaid, That from and after the Ratification of this Act, any White Person or Persons whatsoever, Male or Female, Inhabitant of this Government, or that may or shall remove themselves hither from other Parts, that now is, or hereafter shall be, married with any Negro, Mulatto, Mustee, or other Person being of mixed Blood, as aforesaid, shall be, and are hereby made liable to the same Levies and Taxes, as the Negroes, Mulattoes, or other mixed Blood, as herein above is expressed; [. . .]

Laws, 1723, in Clark, *State Records*, XXIII:106.

The Information of ye Reverend Mr John Blacknall of Edenton in Chowan precinct Clerk taken before Christopher Gale Esq: Cheif Justice of the sayd province this Second day of March one thousand seven hundred & twenty five who sayth that upon the Sayd Second day of March he the sayd John Blacknall did joyn together in the holy estate of Matrimony according to the form of the Church of England in Edenton in Chowan precinct aforesayd Thomas Spencer a White man and a Molatto Woman named Martha paul both of Curratuck precinct contrary to the direction of an Act of Assembly in that case made & provided whereby he the sayd John Blacknall hath incurrd a penalty of fifty pounds the One half to the Informer which he therefore demands the other to be lodged in the hands of the Governor (or Commander in Cheif for the time being) to be applyd according to the directions of the sayd Act.

Signd   JOn BLACKNALL

Subsignd Jurat coramme die & Anno Supradict

C. GALE C. J.

William L. Saunders, ed., *The Colonial Records of North Carolina*, 10 vols. (Raleigh: State of North Carolina, 1886-1890), II:672.

In addressing interracial unions beyond the bounds of marriage, the General Assembly singled out white, female, indentured servants, who might prove vulnerable, willingly or unwillingly, to sexual advances by males, black and white. Trying to discourage the presence of illegitimate children, particularly non-whites, the legislature penalized such mothers by requiring that they be sold by the churchwardens of the local parish for an additional year of service for each white child and two years for each mulatto born out of wedlock. The legislature remained mute on miscegenation that involved black women and white men. Since children assumed the status of their mothers, offspring of slave women were bonded. Male slave owners may well have taken advantage of their bondservants, a practice sufficiently common, even deliberate, in the Lower Cape Fear that it elicited little notice among white North Carolinians. Yet it certainly occasioned reaction from such visitors as Josiah Quincy Jr. and Janet Schaw.

CHAPTER XXIV.

An Act Concerning Servants and Slaves. [. . .]

XVIII. [. . .] And if any White Servant Woman shall, during the Time of her Servitude, be delivered of a Child begotten by any Negro, Mulatto or Indian, such Servant, over and above the Time she is by this Act to serve her Master or Owner for such Offence, shall be sold by the Church Wardens of the Parish, for Two Years, after the Time by Indenture or otherwise is expired: [. . .]

Laws, 1741, in Clark, *State Records*, XXIII:191, 195.

Motion of Alexr. Martin Esqr. Orderd that

Carlotte Diormond a White Woman servant the property of Major John Dunn being brought into Open Court and Charged upon Oath of having two Bastard Children during her Servitude the One a White Child and the other a Mulatto it is adjudged by the Court According to the Act of Assembly in Such Case made and provided that the said

Charlotte diormond after the Expiration of the Term of her said Service by her Indictment shall Serve her Master or his Assigns One Whole year for the Offence of having a White Bastard Child as aforesaid and it is further adjudged that After the Expiration of the said Term of One Year she the said Charlotte Diormond Shall be Sold According to Law to Serve Two Whole Years Longer for the Offence of Having the Mulatto bastard Child as afore said [. . .]

> Minutes of the Rowan County Court of Pleas and Quarter Sessions, February 1769, State Archives, Office of Archives and History, Raleigh.

A mischief incident to both these provinces [North and South Carolina] is very observable, and very natural to be expected — the intercourse between the whites and blacks. The enjoyment of a negro or mulatto woman is spoken of as quite a common thing: no reluctance, delicacy or shame is made about the matter. It is far from being uncommon to see a gentleman at dinner, and his reputed offspring a slave to the master of the table. I myself saw two instances of this, and the company very facetiously would trace the lines, lineaments and features of the father and mother in the child, and very accurately point out the more characteristick resemblance. The fathers neither of them blushed or seem[ed] disconcerted. They were called men of worth, politeness and humanity. Strange perversion of terms and language! The Africans are said to be inferior in point of sense and understanding, sentiment and feeling, to the Europeans and other white nations. Hence the one infer a right to enslave the other. An African Black labors night and day to collect a small pittance to purchase the freedom of his child: the American or European White man begets his likeness and with much indifference and dignity of soul sees his progeny in bondage and misery, and makes not one effort to redeem his own blood. [. . .]

> Mark A. Dewolfe Howe, ed., "The Southern Journal of Josiah Quincy, Junior, 1773," *Proceedings of the Massachusetts Historical Society* 49 (June 1916): 463.

[. . .] Tho' they have fine women and such as might inspire any man with sentiments that do honour to humanity, yet they know no such nice distinctions, and in this at least are real patriots. As the population of the country is all the view they have in what they call love, and tho' they often honour their black wenches with their attention, I sincerely believe they are excited to that crime by no other desire or motive but that of adding to the number of their slaves.

Janet Schaw, *Journal of a Lady of Quality: Being the Narrative of a Journey from Scotland to the West Indies, North Carolina, and Portugal, in the Years 1774 and 1775*, ed. Evangeline W. Andrews and Charles M. Andrews (New Haven: Yale University Press, 1921), 154.

Resistance to Slavery

In countless ways, slaves made known their opposition to bondage. Sarah, a house slave owned by Mrs. Jean Blair, clearly objected to her move from Edenton to a new dwelling in Windsor. Others resorted to theft, necessitated in part by the need to supplement their insufficient food and clothing allowances and in part to obtain goods for use in trade among themselves and with whites. Bondsmen, including Andrew who stole "proc" or proclamation money, well understood the value of paper currency.

Jean Blair to Hannah Iredell

Windsor 24th May 1781

My Dear Sister

I hardly ever knew the trouble of house keeping before, a large family and continual confusion and not any thing to eat but salt meat and hoe cake and no conveniences to dress them. But I hope it will be better soon. Had I none but my own family I should not mind it, but we have never been a day without. I do not think I shall have much less trouble for Sarahs coming up. She thinks herself so ill used to be brought into [Such a mess] before I had prepared a tight house for her with a lock to it and thinks I had more before than I had work for; and I might have learnt them to wash and Iron. She would be bound she could have made out well enough in Edenton, but if she gives herself many more airs she shall never see Edenton again. Very little more will provoke me to sell her. Andrew behaves very well and so does old Simon but Peter seems unwilling to be here and thinks there are enough without him. I daresay it is Sarah that makes him so disatisfied. She never came near me till after repeated messages yesterday to her to come and Iron a few cloaths that were left last week. She made shift to creep here just in the evening and then was very impudent. If she does not behave much better I will hire her here when I do go down if ever I do. [. . .]

Don Higginbotham, ed., *The Papers of James Iredell,* Vol. 2, *1778-1783* (Raleigh: Division of Archives and History, Department of Cultural Resources, 1976), 246-247.

North Carolina Pasquotank County. To Thomas Relfe Special Constable to Execute and make return.

Whereas Complaint hath been made to me one of his Majesties Justices of the peace for the County that a Certain Negroe fellow the property of Mrs. Mary Blount named London And another Negroe fellow the Property of William [Reid] named Dave have on the nights of the 23 and 24th of February last felloniously broke open a Warehouse at Windfield and stole from there Sundry Articles such as Pork Rum and Sugar the property of William McCormick. These are therefore to warrant you to take said Negroes into your Custody and Safely keep untill released under Course of Law Given under my hand and Seal this 2d March 1776.

Thos. Reding J.P. (Seal)

Writ to Thomas Relfe, March 2, 1776, Pasquotank County, Miscellaneous Records, Records of Slaves and Free Persons of Color, Court Actions Involving Slaves, State Archives, Office of Archives and History, Raleigh.

WHEREAS many persons have made it a practice to traffic with the subscriber's negroes, and hunt on his lands, to his great detriment — He therefore gives this public notice, that he is determined to prosecute to the utmost rigour of the law, all those who shall offend herein for the future.

BENJ. WILLIAMS.

State Gazette of North Carolina (New Bern), November 29, 1787.

At a Court Begun and held at the Courthouse in New Bern on Friday the 15th day of October in the Second year of the Reign of our Sovereign Lord George the Third King of Great Britain etc. and in the Year of our Lord one Thousand Seven hundred and Sixty Two for the Tryal of a Certain Negro fellow named Andrew the Property of the Honourable Richard Spaight Esquire Committed for Felony [. . .]

Perigan Cox Swain says that his wife Seen the Prisoner in his room and Asked who was there and then said or Called out at Thief that then the Prisoner Run away and that he lost Twenty or Twenty odd Pounds Proc out of a Desk in the aforesaid Room and that he Believes the Prisoner to be the Person who Stole the aforesaid Sum.

Trial of Andrew, Minutes of the Craven County Court of Pleas and Quarter Sessions, October 17, 1762, State Archives, Office of Archives and History, Raleigh.

Some slaves resorted to more destructive actions to protest their bondage. Particularly threatening was the use of poison, for a knowledge of plants and their powers allowed slaves a subtle means of venting their anger that was difficult to detect. Arson, like poisoning, was hard to prove; though when caught, Toney in Rowan County defiantly admitted his crime. Other slaves retaliated more directly, attacking those who had mistreated them: in the murder of Henry Ormond, they refused their master any mercy as it allegedly had not been shown to them.

Mary Ward, administratrix of Benjamin Ward, of Onslow county, deceased, was allowed her claim of sixty pounds for negro condemned and executed for poisoning of his late master, as per certificate filed [. . .]

Reports of the Committee of Public Claims, House of Commons, December 11, 1770, in Walter Clark, ed., *The State Records of North Carolina*, 16 vols. (11-26) (Raleigh: State of North Carolina, 1895-1906), XXII:856.

February 7th 1777

State of North Carolina Rowan County.

It being Certified by the Sheriff of said County to Robert King Esquire one of the Justices of the said County that Toney a Negroe man Slave the property of Walter Sharp of the County aforesaid had been Committed to, and is now, confined in Jail for maliciously voluntarily and feloniously, burning the Dwelling house of said Walter, the said Robert King issued a Summons agreeable to Law for two Justices and four Freeholders to appear at Salisbury this day for the Tryal of said Negroe (to wit) for Matthew Troy and Christopher Beekman Justices, William Nessbit, Alexander Dobbins, James Brandon and John Stone, Freeholders and owners of Slaves in said County. The aforesaid Justices and Freeholders having met as a Court proceeded to examine said negroe Toney, who on his Examination Acknowledged in plain and manifest Terms That he the said Toney did set fire to, and burn the Dwelling house of the aforementioned Walter Sharp, without any other Reasons prompting him thereto but his own evil mind. The Court thereupon find the said Toney guilty in manner and form as above charged, The said negroe Toney being asked by the Court whether he had any Reasons to offer to the Court why Sentence of Death should not be passed upon him, and he answered that he had none, [. . .]

Trial of Toney, February 7, 1777, Minutes of the Rowan County Court of Pleas and Quarter Sessions, State Archives, Office of Archives and History, Raleigh. Toney was hung.

NEWBERN, *August* 3.

A FEW weeks ago, we published an account from Beaufort county, of the murder of Mr. Henry Ormond, by his own slaves; since which we have received a true account of that tragical affair, which has been discovered by the confession of one of the slaves in the conspiracy: Five of them conspired against their master, and on the Sunday night he was said to have rode from home in quest of one of his slaves who was missing, the conspirators, after their master was a bed, went up to his room, and with an handkerchief attempted to strangle him, which they thought they had effected, but in a little time after they had left him, he recovered, and began to stir, on hearing which they went up again, and told him he must die, and that before they left the room; he begged very earnestly for his life, but one of them, his house wench, told him it was in vain, that as he had no mercy on them, he could expect none himself, and immediately threw him between two feather beds, and all got on him till he was stifled to death. [. . .]

Virginia Gazette (Williamsburg: Rind), September 6, 1770.

Slaves also manifested their rebelliousness by running away, a serious crime that not only deprived owners of their labor but also threatened the security of the white community. Most runaways were young adults, usually American-born blacks who had acquired some command of the English language, possessed a ready skill, and had been accustomed to dealing with whites. Many, like rivermen, had enjoyed latitude of movement by their masters. A small number had been born in Africa and immediately sought their freedom upon arrival in the colony. Harsh treatment as indicated by scarification, the desire to join spouses or kinsmen, and the primal instinct for liberty impelled slaves to "steal themselves."

RUN *away from the subscriber some time in November last, a tall negro fellow called Jamey; speaks good English, and had on when he went away, a new suit of cloaths made of white negro cloth,* [. . .]

James Moore.

Cape Fear Mercury (Wilmington), January 13, 1773.

Newbern, February 20, 1775.

ONE HUNDRED AND TEN POUNDS REWARD.

ABSENTED themselves very early on *Sunday* Morning the 19th Instant, from the House of the Subscribers, Five newly imported Slaves, (Four Men and One Woman:) Two of the Men, named *Kanchee* and *Boohum*, are Six Feet One or Two inches high, and about 30 Years of Age; another named *Ji*, is near Five Feet Nine Inches high, and about 25 Years of Age, has sore Eyes; and the Fourth, named *Sambo Pool*, is a short well set Fellow, aged 18 Years; the Woman, named *Peg Manny*, is of short Stature and elderly. The Fellows were uniformly clad in coarse green Cloth Jackets, brown Cloth Trowsers, a Blanket, and red Cloth Cap; and the Wench had on an emboss'd Flannel Petticoat and brown Cloth Cloak. [. . .] they are incapable of uttering a Word of *English*, have been extremely well-fed, and very little worked, [. . .]

North Carolina Gazette (New Bern), February 24, 1775.

September 24, 1791

Five Pounds Reward.

RAN away from the subscriber on the 17th of August last, a likely young negro man named JAMES, about 21 years of age, five feet 7, or 8 inches high, of a yellowish complexion, by trade a blacksmith; most used to making axes, he stoops forward in his knees and body as if he had a burthen on his back—his back is marked with the whip, he has a scar on one of his elbows occasioned by a burn; has small legs and very large feet—has a bold look, speaks good English and can tell a smooth tale—born on Trent river.—[. . .]

AARON LAMBERT.

Advertisement in *North Carolina Gazette, or Impartial Intelligencer and Weekly Advertiser* (New Bern), in Freddie L. Parker, ed., *Stealing a Little Freedom: Advertisements for Slave Runaways in North Carolina, 1791-1840* (New York: Garland Publishing Co., 1994), 3.

June 13, 1796

RAN away from the subscriber on the 21st instant, a likely negro man named BOB — about 26 years of age, 6 feet high, stout made, black complected, and a little bow-leg'd; had on when he went away, a white negro cotton jacket, and green trousers, and took a number of other clothes with him — it is probable he is aiming for Cumberland, as his wife belongs to Major John Baker, who has lately removed from this county to that place. [. . .]

ROBERT PARKER.

Gates county, May 24th, 1796.

Advertisement in *North Carolina Journal* (Halifax), in Parker, *Stealing a Little Freedom*, 53.

———————

Fugitives in North Carolina found refuge in North Carolina's many swamps. Vast, impenetrable wastelands like Great Dismal Swamp, that straddled the North Carolina-Virginia border, and Great Alligator Swamp, between Albemarle Sound and the Pamlico River, offered sanctuaries where whites rarely ventured. Low-lying areas in the Lower Cape Fear also served as hideaways. Slaves in the northern counties often escaped to Virginia; others tried to leave North Carolina by boat, either stowing away or enlisting the aid of sympathetic captains or crew.

This one first mentioned is also called the *Great Alligator dismal Swamp*, and lies between those two vast expanses of water, or rather seas, named Pamphlico and Albemarle Sounds. [. . .]

Run-away Negroes have resided in these places for twelve, twenty, or thirty years and upwards, subsisting themselves in the swamp upon corn, hogs, and fowls, that they raised on some of the spots not perpetually under water, nor subject to be flooded, as forty-nine parts out of fifty of it are; and on such spots they have erected habitations, and cleared small fields around them; yet these have always been perfectly impenetrable to any of the inhabitants of the country around, even to those nearest to and best acquainted with the swamps.[. . .]

John F. D. Smyth, *A Tour in the United States of America*, 2 vols. (1784; reprint, New York: Arno Press, 1968), 2:100, 102.

WILMINGTON, July 2.

In the night of the 26th ult. a very daring robbery was committed in the lower part of this town, upon the warehouse or cellar under the dwelling-house of Thomas Maclaine, Esq.

The villains having forced open the door of the same with an iron instrument, took thereout, and carried off in boats which they had previously provided for the purpose, one hogshead of tobacco, a hogshead of Molasses, and two barrels of beef.

In consequence of a strict search being made, in the morning of the 28th ult. the whole of the stolen property was found in a place of concealment upon Barnets Creek, about a mile from the entrance to it.

This place appeared to have been long a camp or asylum for runaway negroes, and probably was generally the repository for the goods which have been stolen in this town for some time past, by them and their confederates.

It is situated in a swamp, and contains about an acre of cleared ground, which is planted with corn. Some [huts] were upon the place; and several hoes, axes, and cooking materials were found, as well as instruments for breaking locks, &c. — and from the fires that were burning and other circumstances it was evident, the possessors had fled very precipitately upon the first alarm of a discovery.

Wilmington Centinel, and General Advertiser, July 2, 1788.

May 16, 1745
Virginia Gazette

North-Carolina, April 24, 1745.

RAN away, on the 18th Instant, from the Plantation of the late Col. *William Wilson*, deceas'd, Two Slaves belonging to the Subscriber, the one a tall yellow Fellow, named *Emanuel*, about 6 Feet high, six or seven and Twenty Years of Age; hath a Scar on the outside of his left Thigh, which was cut with an Ax; he had on when he went away, a blue Jacket, an Ozenbrig Shirt and Trousers, and a Worsted Cap; he speaks pretty good *English*, and calls himself a *Portugueze*; is by Trade a Cooper, and took with him some Cooper's Tools. The other is a short, thick, well-set Fellow, stoops forward pretty much as he walks; does not speak so plain as the other; had on when he went away an Ozenbrig Pair of Trousers and Shirt, a white Negro Cotton Jacket, and took with him an Axe: They went away in a small Cannoe, and were seen at Capt. *Pearson*'s, on *Nuse* River, the 18th Inst. and 'tis believ'd are gone towards *Virginia*. Whoever takes up the said Negros, and brings them to my

House on *Trent* River, *North-Carolina*, or secures them so that I may have them again, shall have Four Pistoles Reward for each, paid by

Mary Wilson.

Virginia Gazette (Williamsburg: Parks), May 16, 1745.

CHAP. V.

An Act *to amend an act, entitled,* An act to prevent the stealing of slaves, or by violence, seduction or any other means taking or carrying away any slave or slaves the property of another, and for other purposes therein mentioned.

WHEREAS the above recited act hath been found insufficient to prevent the iniquitous practice of carrying and conveying slaves out of this state:

I. *Be it enacted by the General Assembly of the state of North-Carolina, and it is hereby enacted by the authority of the same,* That from and after the passing of this act, if any master or commander of any ship or vessel trading within this state, shall carry and convey out of the same on board of any such ship or vessel any negro or mulatto slave or slaves, the property of any citizen or citizens of this state, without the consent in writing of the owner or owners, his, her or their guardian or guardians of such slave or slaves previously obtained; or shall take and receive on board of any such vessel or ship, any such slave or slaves, or permit or suffer the same to be done with the intent and for the purpose of carrying and conveying such slave or slaves out of this state, or shall wickedly and willingly conceal or permit to be concealed on board of any such ship or vessel any negro or mulatto slave or slaves, who shall or may hereafter abscond from his, her or their master or mistress, being citizens of this state, with the intent and for the purpose of enabling such slave or slaves to effect his, her or their escape out of this state, every such master or commander of any such ship or vessel so carrying and conveying, or so taking or receiving or concealing, or causing or permiting the same to be done with an intent as aforesaid, shall be deemed and taken to be guilty of felony, and shall suffer death as a felon without benefit of clergy.

Laws of the State of North-Carolina, 1792, c. 5.

86

Slave owners used various means to apprehend runaways. Jacob Wilkinson sought assistance from acquaintances and friends. Others hired Indians as slave catchers. The numerous newspaper advertisements that attested to the frequency of runaways usually contained pertinent information that might identify the slaves, including distinctive physical characteristics. Some owners attempted to surmise the destination of runaways based on previous ownership and family connections. All whites were directed by law to capture runaways and slaves without proper identification.

Wilmington 29th Novemr. 1766

Dr. Sr. [. . .]

My Negro Fellow Jack, is runaway and undoubtedly is gone up to his old range Pray have him taken up and Sent Safe down, Sepose he Will Endeavour to Keep out of the Way; but am Certain you can Scheame so as to have him apprehended, I was told when I bought him that he was about getting a Molatto wench of Jeff Williams for a Wife [. . .]

> Jacob Wilkinson to "Dear Sir," November 29, 1766, McAllister Papers, Southern Historical Collection, Manuscripts Department, Wilson Library, University of North Carolina at Chapel Hill.

The *Negroes* sometimes make use of these Advantages in the Woods, where they will stay for Months together before they can be found out by their Masters, or any other Person; and great Numbers of them would act after the same manner (which would be detrimental to the Planters) were they not so much afraid of the *Indians*, who have such a natural aversion to the *Blacks*, that they commonly shoot them when ever they find them in the Woods or solitary parts of the Country.

> John Brickell, *The Natural History of North Carolina* (1737; reprint, Murfreesboro, N.C.: Johnson Publishing Co., 1968), 263.

[1715] The Examination of John Tate, Labourer, brought before Christor Gale Esqr., Chief Justice of North Carolina for Felony and Burglary,

"Saith, That about eight weeks agone he confederating with John Fenix calling himself a free negro, and young Tony & Moses Slaves of Mr. Tookes, went away from Mr. Tookes plantation, in a Cannoe of the said Tookes, that as they went they put ashore at Majr Hecklefields &

took into their Company one Jane Fenix als Anderson then under Custody of the Marshall for Suspicion of Murder [. . .]"

"Mr. Jno. Taneyhill Saith That on ye 20 or 21st of March that he with William Dupuis & two Indians (being Requested by Mr. James Tookes to apprehend John Tate &c. for Felony & Burglary) he came up with the said John Fenix, Jane Fenix als Anderson at ye Edge of a great Pocoson between Neus & Newport Rivers in Bath County. That they there apprehended them with the goods now produced and brought them in. [. . .]"

James Robert Bent Hathaway, ed., *North Carolina Historical and Genealogical Register*, 3 vols. (Edenton: 1900-1903), III: 285.

CABIN POINT, *June* 26, 1771.

RUN away from the Subscriber's Plantation in *Bute* County, *North Carolina*, some Time in *July* last, a Negro Fellow named WILL. He is about thirty eight Years of Age, thick set, and well made, much scared with Whipping, and one of his great Toes off, I believe, at the second Joint. He formerly belonged to Colonel *John Tabb*, deceased, of *Elizabeth City*, and is supposed to be lurking in that Neighbourhood, or that of Mrs. *Lydia Jones* of the said County, who owns a Brother to the said Negro. FORTY SHILLINGS Reward, besides what the Law allows, will be given for apprehending and securing him in any of his Majesty's Jails, or FIVE POUNDS if he be taken out of the Colony. [. . .]

JOHN AUSTIN FINNIE.

Virginia Gazette (Williamsburg: Purdie and Dixon), July 4, 1771.

CHAPTER XLVI.

An Act Concerning Servants & Slaves. [. . .]

IX. And Be It Further Enacted that all persons shall use their utmost endeavours to apprehend all such Servants & Slaves as they conceive to be Runaways or travell without Tickett as afors'd or that shall be seen off his Master's ground Arm'd with any Gun, Sword or any other Weapon of defence or offence altho' provided with a Tickett unless particularly mentioned and him, her or them having Apprehended shall carry & convey before the next Magistrate which Magistrate is hereby impowered to order and adjudge such Corporal Punishment to the said suspected Runaway as he shall think fitt [. . .]

Laws of North Carolina, 1715, in Clark, *State Records*, XXIII:62, 63.

Runaways who refused to submit and constituted a danger to society risked outlawry. The North Carolina slave code of 1715, closely following a Virginia statute of 1691, required that two justices of the peace sign an affidavit of outlawry after which the transgressors might be apprehended by any means necessary. Outlaws or not, some slaves refused to be taken. Phillis was shot and York drowned in efforts to thwart their captors.

ACT XVI.

An act for suppressing outlying Slaves.

WHEREAS many times negroes, mulattoes, and other slaves unlawfully absent themselves from their masters and mistresses service, and lie hid and lurk in obscure places killing hoggs and committing other injuries to the inhabitants of this dominion, for remedy whereof for the future, *Be it enacted by their majesties lieutenant governour, councell and burgesses of this present generall assembly, and the authoritie thereof, and it is hereby enacted,* that in all such cases upon intelligence of any such negroes, mulattoes, or other slaves lying out, two of their majesties justices of the peace of that county, whereof one to be of the quorum, where such negroes, mulattoes or other slave shall be, shall be impowered and commanded, and are hereby impowered and commanded to issue out their warrants directed to the sherrife of the same county to apprehend such negroes, mulattoes, and other slaves, which said sherriffe is hereby likewise required upon all such occasions to raise such and soe many forces from time to time as he shall think convenient and necessary for the effectual apprehending such negroes, mulattoes and other slaves, and in case any negroes, mulattoes or other slave or slaves lying out as aforesaid shall resist, runaway, or refuse to deliver and surrender him or themselves to any person or persons that shall be by lawfull authority employed to apprehend and take such negroes, mulattoes or other slaves that in such cases it shall and may be lawfull for such person and persons to kill and distroy such negroes, mulattoes, and other slave or slaves by gunn or any otherwaise whatsoever.

Laws, 1691, in William Waller Hening, ed., *The Statutes at Large; Being a Collection of All the Laws of Virginia*, 13 vols., 2d ed. (Philadelphia: the editor, by Thomas Desilver, 1823), III:86.

CHAPTER XXIV.

An Act Concerning Servants and Slaves. [. . .]

XLV. And whereas many Times Slaves run away and lie out hid and lurking in the Swamps, Woods and other Obscure Places, killing Cattle and Hogs, and committing other Injuries to the Inhabitants in this Government: Be it therefore Enacted, by the Authority aforesaid, That in all such Cases, upon Intelligence of any Slave or Slaves lying out as aforesaid, any Two Justices of the Peace for the County wherein such Slave or Slaves is or are supposed to lurk to do Mischief, shall, and they are hereby impowered and required, to issue Proclamation against such Slave or Slaves (reciting his or their Name or Names, and the Name or Names of the Owner or Owners, if known), thereby requiring him or them, and every of them, forthwith to surrender him or themselves; and also, to impower and require the Sheriff of the said County to take such Power with him as he shall think fit and necessary for going in search and pursuit of and effectual apprehending such outlying Slave or Slaves; [. . .] And if any Slave or Slaves against whom Proclamation hath been thus issued, stay out and do not immediately return home, it shall be lawful for any Person or Persons whatsoever to kill and destroy such Slave or Slaves by such Ways and Means as he or she shall think fit, without Accusation or Impeachment of any Crime for the same.

XLVI. Provided always, and it is further Enacted, That for every Slave killed in Pursuance of this Act, or put to Death by Law, the Master or Owner of such Slave shall be paid by the Public; and all Tryals of Slaves for Capital or other Crimes, shall be in the Manner and according as hereinafter is directed.

Laws, 1715, in Clark, *State Records*, XXIII:191, 201, 202.

CRAVEN COUNTY, ss.

By JAMES DAVIS *and* THOMAS HASLEN, *Esquires, Two of his Majesty's Justices of the Peace for said County.*

WHEREAS Complaint hath been made to us, by *John Kennedy*, that a Negro Fellow belonging to him, named ABRAHAM, between 20 & 21 Years old, a short well-made Fellow, has a Scar over one of his Eyes, had on a Flannel Shirt, and a Pair of Osnabrug Breeches, ran away from him about the 1st of *June* last, and is supposed to be lurking about, committing many Acts of Felony.

THESE are therefore, in his Majesty's Name, to command the said Slave forthwith to surrender himself, and return home to his said Master. And we do hereby also require the Sheriff of the said County of *Craven*, to make diligent Search and Pursuit after the above mentioned Slave, and him having found, to apprehend and secure, so that he may be conveyed to his said Master, or otherwise discharged as the Law directs; and the said Sheriff is hereby impowered to raise and take with him such Power of this County as he shall think fit, for apprehending the said Slave. And we do hereby, by Virtue of an Act of Assembly of this Province concerning Servants and Slaves, intimate and declare, if the said *Abraham* doth not surrender himself, and return home, immediately after the Publication of these Presents, that any Person may kill and destroy the said Slave, by such Means as he or they may think fit, without Accusation or Impeachment of any Crime or Offence for so doing, or without incurring any Penalty or Forfeiture thereby.

GIVEN under our Hands and Seals, this 12*th Day of* August, 1774, *and in the* 14*th Year of his Majesty's Reign.*

JAMES DAVIS,
THOMAS HASLEN.

N.B. Whoever brings the said Slave to me alive, shall have 40s. and 5l. for his Head.

JOHN KENNEDY.

North Carolina Gazette (New Bern), September 2, 1774.

We whose names are underwritten being Summons'd as a Jury of Inquest, and being duly Sworn on the Holy Evangelist on the 3d Day of February 1768 to View the Body of a Negroe Wench, (Supposd to be the property of James Hasell Esqr.) which was Shot and Since died in the Goal of Wilmington, are Unanimisly of Opineon that She died in Consequence of the said Wound, Given under our Hands and Seals the day and year above Written [. . .]

Wilmington 30th October 1768 These are to Certify the above is a True Coppy of Inquest taken before me . . .

Jno. Quince Corroner [. . .]

North Carolina. New Hanover County.

These may Certify to whome It may Concern That I was one of The Justices who signed [a host] Lawyers for a Negro wench Named Phillis Belonging To the Honorable James Hassell Esqr. which Negro wench was afterwards shott In the [*incomplete*] Taken as I was Informed.

Fredk. Gregg

Wilmington 31st Octobr. 1768

Inquest, October 30, 1768, Affidavit of Frederick Gregg, October 31, 1768, New Hanover County, Miscellaneous Records, Coroners' Inquests, State Archives, Office of Archives and History, Raleigh.

It appearing to the Court that a Certain Negroe Slave Named York belonging to Richard Hall being Outlawed and in pursuit was Drowned. [. . .]

Minutes of the Craven County Court of Pleas and Quarter Sessions, December 1770, State Archives.

While countless numbers of runaways found their freedom by hiding out in swamps or passing as free in North Carolina and elsewhere, others were not so fortunate. Abraham was apprehended. Harry claimed that his master had died, after which the slave wandered about and eventually submitted to whites. Two recently imported slaves, who apparently had been jailed after absconding and had suffered terrible privation, managed to free themselves and make their way to the kitchen of Robert Williams, who cared for them in their pitiable condition.

TAKEN up by the subscriber in New-Hanover county on the North-East of Cape-Fear river in North-Carolina, a new-negro man, calls himself Abraham, he is about 5 feet 7 inches high, between 25 and 30 years of age, with his upper teeth fil'd; had on a negro-cloth jacket and trousers, speaks but very little English. The owner is desired to come and prove his property with paying all charges to

JOHN BUFORD.
September 21, 1773.

Cape Fear Mercury (Wilmington), September 22, 1773.

CAME to the Subscribers Plantation on Sunday last, a Negro Fellow, who says his Name is HARRY. — He speaks very broken, & can give no account where he came from:— He says his Master is dead:— He appears to be about 30 years of age, thick set, and 5 feet high. — Whoever will prove said Negro to be their Property and pay Charges, may have again by applying to

EDWARD RUSSEL,
(Living on the Sound.

Wilmington, October 13.

Wilmington Centinel, and General Advertiser, October 15, 1788.

TAKEN up and commited to Goal at *Beaufort* in *Carteret* County, Two new Negroes, they came in a Canoe to *Bogue* Sound, but where from we cannot understand. By some Accident, or Act of Humanity, they got out of Goal, of a cold Evening (almost starved even in the fore part of the Night, and must have inevitably perished before Morning) and Strayed to the Subscriber's Kitchen, who wishes the proper Owner had them, but cannot send them any more into Confinement to starve and freeze to Death according to Law: For the Great Law-Giver *Moses*, had in Command, that we should do no Murder.

ROBERT WILLIAMS.

Hamlet, Carteret County,
Nov. 22, 1773.

North Carolina Gazette (New Bern), January 7, 1774.

———————————

Although individuals like Williams informed the public of the apprehension of runaway slaves, North Carolina law, which paralleled a 1705 Virginia act, required that captured runaways be remanded to the custody of the county sheriff. That official in turn advertised the slaves in hopes of locating the owners. In the interim, the slaves might be hired out, during which time they were forced to wear an iron collar marked P(ublic) G(aol) in order to absolve public officials of any responsibility in the event of their escape.

XXIII. And for encouragement of all persons to take up runaways, *Be it enacted, by the authority aforesaid, and it is hereby enacted,* That for the taking up of every servant, or slave, if ten miles, or above, from the house or quarter where such servant, or slave was kept, there shall be allowed by the public, as a reward to the taker-up, two hundred pounds of tobacco; and if above five miles, and under ten, one hundred pounds of tobacco: [. . .]

XXIV. *Provided,* That when any negro, or other runaway, that doth not speak English, and cannot, or through obstinacy will not, declare the name of his or her masters or owner, that then it shall be sufficient for the said justice to certify the same, instead of the name of such runaway, and the proper name and sur-name of his or her master or owner, and the county of his or her residence and distance of miles, as aforesaid; and in such case, shall, by his warrant, order the said runaway to be conveyed to the public gaol, of this country, there to be continued prisoner until the master or owner shall be known; who, upon paying the charges of the imprisonment, or giving caution to the prison-keeper for the same, together with the reward of two hundred or one hundred pounds of tobacco, as the case shall be, shall have the said runaway restored.

Laws, 1705, in Hening, *The Statutes at Large; . . . Virginia,* V:455-456.

CHAPTER XXIV.

An Act Concerning Servants and Slaves. [. . .]

XXIX. And be it further Enacted, by the Authority aforesaid, That if any Negro or other Person, who shall be taken up as a Runaway and brought before any Justice of the Peace, and cannot speak English, or through Obstinacy, will not declare the name of his or her Owner, such Justice shall in such Case, and he is hereby required, by a Warrant under his Hand, to commit the said Negro, Slave or Runaway to the Gaol of the County wherein he or she shall be taken up; and the Sheriff or Under-Sheriff of the County into whose Custody the said Runaway shall be committed, shall forthwith cause Notice, in Writing, of such Commitment to be set up on the Court-house Door of the said County, and there continued during the Space of Two Months; [. . .]

XXXI. And be it further Enacted, by the Authority aforesaid, That when any Negro or Runaway, as aforesaid, shall be delivered to the Keeper of the Public Gaol of this Government by Virtue of this Act, and his or her Master or Owner cannot be known, it shall and may be lawful for the Keeper of the said Gaol, upon his application to the General Court, or the nearest County Court to the said Gaol, or to any

Two Justices, out of the Court, with the Consent of either of the said Courts, or Two Justices, as aforesaid, to let the said Negro or Runaway to Hire, to any Person or Persons whom they shall approve of, for such Sum or Sums of Money, or Quantity of Commodities, and for such Term or Time, as they shall direct; [. . .]

XXXIII. And be it further Enacted, by the Authority aforesaid, That when the Keeper of the said Public Gaol shall, by Direction of such Court as aforesaid, let out any Negro or Runaway to Hire to any Person or Persons whomseover, the said Keeper shall, at the Time of his Delivery, cause an iron Collar to be put on the Neck of such Negro or Runaway with the Letters P.G. stamped thereon; and that thereafter the said Keeper shall not be answerable for the Escape of the said Negro or Runaway.

Laws, 1741, in Clark, *State Records*, XXIII:191, 198, 199.

Orderd that a certain runaway negroe Man committed to the Goal of this County be hired to Captain John Smith which is agreed to by the said John Smith at the rate of Fifteen shillings per Month to pay the Fees due the sheriff and Goaler and that the said John Smith do put an Iron Collar round his Neck mark'd with the Letters P.G.

Minutes of the Chowan County Court of Pleas and Quarter Sessions, December 1772, State Archives, Office of Archives and History, Raleigh.

———————

The most threatening form of slave discontent was organized opposition that might lead to concerted attacks on whites and, possibly, insurrection. The slave code deemed bondsmen, who gathered in groups of three or more for such purposes, guilty of felony. A large body of slaves roamed New Hanover County in 1767. Less than a decade later the onset of the Revolution seemed to inspire unrest among eastern North Carolina slaves, who perhaps tried to emulate their masters' own quest for separation from Great Britain. The New Bern Committee of Safety believed that royal governor Josiah Martin would follow the example of his counterpart in Virginia, Lord Dunmore, by arming slaves and granting them freedom in order to help defeat the colonial challenge to British authority. At the same time, slaves were restive in the area around Wilmington. Whites reacted quickly and decisively to thwart any incipient insurrections.

CHAPTER XXIV.

An Act Concerning Servants and Slaves. [. . .]

XLVII. And be it further Enacted, by the Authority aforesaid, That if any Number of Negroes or other Slaves, that is to say, Three or more, shall at any Time hereafter, consult, advise or conspire to rebell, or make insurrection, or shall plot or conspire the Murther of any Person or Persons whatsoever, every such consulting, plotting, or conspiring, shall be adjudged and deemed Felony; And the Slave or Slaves convicted thereof, in Manner hereafter directed, shall suffer Death.

Laws, 1741, in Clark, *State Records*, XXIII:191, 202.

The Court being informd that upwards of Twenty runaway Slaves in abody Arm'd, and are now in this County.

Order'd that the Sheriff do immediately raise the power of the County not to be less than Thirty Men well arm'd, to go in pursuit of the said runaway Slaves and that the said Sheriff be impowerd to Shoot Kill and destroy all such of the said runaway Slaves as shall not Surrender themselves.

Minutes of the New Hanover County Court of Pleas and Quarter Sessions, June 1767, State Archives, Office of Archives and History, Raleigh.

Proceedings of the Safety Committee at New Bern.

COMMITTEE CHAMBER, August 2d, 1775. [. . .]

Resolved unanimously, That notwithstanding the very great pains that have been taken by those who call themselves friends to Government, and their favorable explanations of the emphatical words between turned commas in the body of the above Letter, to make them speak a language different from their true import, they contain, in plain English, and in every construction of language, a justification of the design of encouraging the slaves to revolt, when every other means should fail to preserve the King's Government from open and declared rebellion; and the publick avowal of a crime of so horrid and truly black a complexion, could only originate in a soul lost to every sense of the feelings of humanity, and long hackneyed in the detestable and wicked purpose of subjugating these Colonies to the most abject slavery.

By order   R. COGDELL, Chairman.

William L. Saunders, ed., *The Colonial Records of North Carolina*, 10 vols. (Raleigh: State of North Carolina, 1886-1890), X:137, 138a.

[July 1775]. I came to town yesterday with an intention of being at church this day, where I was informed there was to be service performed by a very good clergyman. In this however I was disappointed, for I found the whole town in an uproar, and the moment I landed, Mr Rutherfurd's negroes were seized and taken into custody till I was ready to return with them. This apparent insult I resented extremely, till going up to Doctor Cobham's, I found my short prophecy in regard to the Negroes was already fulfilled and that an insurrection was hourly expected. There had been a great number of them discovered in the adjoining woods the night before, most of them with arms, and a fellow belonging to Doctor Cobham was actually killed. All parties are now united against the common enemies. Every man is in arms and the patroles going thro' all the town, and searching every Negro's house, to see they are all at home by nine at night. [. . .]

Janet Schaw, *Journal of a Lady of Quality: Being the Narrative of a Journey from Scotland to the West Indies, North Carolina, and Portugal, in the Years 1774 and 1775,* ed. Evangeline W. Andrews and Charles M. Andrews (New Haven: Yale University Press, 1921), 199-200.

———————————

As indicated by Martin's alleged scheme, the American Revolution constituted an unprecedented opportunity for slaves to obtain their freedom. When the British military appeared in North Carolina, both in the spring of 1776 and during the invasion of the state in 1780-1781, slaves availed themselves of the chance to flee. Several went to British ships stationed in the Cape Fear River in the early years of the war, and many subsequently enlisted in the service of the British navy and army, including London, a slave of Isaac DuBois. A few served in loyalist militia units in North Carolina. Most participated as noncombatants in the British army. General Charles Cornwallis used blacks as foragers. Though under strict discipline, the African Americans excited near panic among whites in the Edenton vicinity as they approached.

List of Negroes, March 3, 1776, who fled to HMS *Scorpion*

No	Entry.	Year	Appearance	Place and County where Born
[...]				
3	4 [March]	[1776]	4 [March]	Negroes fled For Protection
4				
5				
6				
7				
8	5 [March]		5 [March]	
9				
10				
11				
12	6 [March]		6 [March]	
13				
14				
15	7 [March]		7 [March]	
16				
17				
18	8 March	1776	March 8th	Negroes fled For Protection
19	[8 March]	[1776]	[March 8th]	
22	10 [March]	[1776]	[March] 10	
23	[10 March]	[1776]	[March 10]	
39	1 May	[1776]	May 1	
40	1 June	[1776]	June 1st	
41	[1 June]	[1776]	[June 1st]	
42	[1 June]	[1776]	[June 1st]	
43	[1 June]	[1776]	[June 1st]	
44	[1 June]	[1776]	[June 1st]	

List of Negroes, March 3, 1776, who fled to HMS *Scorpion*

	MENS NAMES	D. D.D. Or R.	Time of Discharge	Year	Whither or for what Reason
[3]	Abraham	D	21 May	[1776]	on Service No. Carolina per Order Sir P[eter] Parker
[4]	Murphy	D	[21 May]	[1776]	[on Service No. Carolina per Order Sir Peter Parker]
[5]	Dick 1st				
[6]	Thom 1				
[7]	John 1				
[8]	Abberdeen				
[9]	Gilbert	D	21st May	1776	On Service No. Carolina per Order Sir Peter Parker
[10]	Goosman	D	[21st May]	[1776]	[On Service No. Carolina per Order Sir Peter Parker]
[11]	Bobb	D	[21st May]	[1776]	[On Service No. Carolina per Order Sir Peter Parker]
[12]	Fryday	D	[21st May]	[1776]	[On Service No. Carolina per Order Sir Peter Parker]
[13]	Quash	D	[21st May]	[1776]	[On Service No. Carolina per Order Sir Peter Parker]
[14]	Morris	D	[21st May]	[1776]	[On Service No. Carolina per Order Sir Peter Parker]
[15]	Thom 2	D	[21st May]	[1776]	[On Service No. Carolina per Order Sir Peter Parker]
[16]	Ben	D	[21st May]	[1776]	[On Service No. Carolina per Order Sir Peter Parker]
[17]	John 2	D	[21st May]	[1776]	[On Service No. Carolina per Order Sir Peter Parker]
[18]	Dick 2nd	D	21st May	1776	On Service No. Carolina per Order Sir P[eter] Parker
[19]	Betty	D	[21st May]	[1776]	[On Service No. Carolina per Order Sir Peter Parker]
[22]	Jacob	D	[21st May]	[1776]	[On Service No. Carolina per Order Sir Peter Parker]
[23]	James	D	[21st May]	[1776]	[On Service No. Carolina per Order Sir Peter Parker]
[39]	Willm. Orrock				
[40]	Henry Grange				
[41]	Abraham Grange				
[42]	Peter Grange				
[43]	Geo. Bryan				
[44]	Willm. Daniel				

List of blacks who fled to HMS *Scorpion*, March 3, 1776, in Admiralty 36/8377. British Records, State Archives, Office of Archives and History, Raleigh. The column headed "D., D. D., Or R" indicates persons who were "Discharged," "Discharged, Died," or "Run away" from the ship.

Office of American Claims
27 May 1789

Present
Mr. Pemberton
Mr. Mackenzie

Examination on the Demand of Lieutenant Isaac Du Bois late of North Carolina.

Demand
For the Value of a Mulatto Slave............£100
Nine years Loss of his Labour 180

Memorial read Stating

That in the Year 1776 a Mulatto Slave named London by Trade a Baker the property of the Memorialist joined the Kings Troops at Cape Fear in North Carolina, was taken into the Service by Order of Sir Henry Clinton, and inrolled in a Company of Black Pioneers under the Command of Captain George Martin by which Service the Said Slave became intitled to his Freedom and Memorialist deprived of him — that his intrinsic Worth was £100 Sterling and the Loss of his Labor for nine Years £180 which is less than half of the Common Wages: prays payment accordingly of £280 Sterling.

Loyalist Claim of Isaac DuBois, 1789, in Audit Office 12/73. British Records, State Archives, Office of Archives and History, Raleigh.

HEAD Qrs. HARRISONS HOUSE,
12th. Jany. 1781. [. . .]

A Return to be given in immedy of the Number of Negroes, Male & Female, attach'd to Each Corps and Departmts. also the No. of Horses, Specifying for Officers & those for Waggons. No Negroes to be permitted to follow the Army who do not Wear a Mark to distinguish the Corps they belong to. [. . .]

HEAD Qrs. SALISBURY,
5th Feb: 1781 [. . .]

Great Complaints having been made of Negroes Stragling from the Line of March, plundrg & Using Violence to the Inhabitants It is Lord Cornwallis possitive Orders that no Negroe shall be Suffred to Carry Arms on any pretence & all Offrs. & other persons who Employ Negroes are desir'd to acqt. them that the Provt. Marshall has recd Ordrs. to Seize & punish on the Spot any Negroe follg the Army who may Offend against this regulation.

Albert R. Newsome, ed., "A British Orderly Book, 1780-1781," *North Carolina Historical Review* 9 (July 1932): 279-280, 296.

Jean Blair to James Iredell

Windsor 21st July 1781

Dear Sir

Billy Blair came from Edenton yesterday. He says every Body there was marching out to endeavour to surprise six hundred Negroes who were sent out by L Cornwallis to plunder and get provisions. It is said they have no Arms but what they find in the houses they plunder. When they applyed for arms they were told they had no occasion for any as they were not to go to any place where any number of Rebels were collected. It is said there are two thousand of them out in different Partys. [. . .]

Higgenbotham, *Iredell Papers*, II:266.

———————

Although the yoke of slavery remained firmly fastened upon most blacks after the Revolution, the lessons and success of the white colonial liberation movement were not lost upon bondsmen. Slaves in New Bern and its vicinity may have attempted a concerted effort to gain their freedom in 1792, as did those in Bertie County in 1798. Most poignantly, rebellious African

Americans showed an understanding of white military and political organization. One runaway in the Lower Cape Fear styled himself "General." Another, Quillo in Granville County, tried to establish a polity among slaves, based on the principle of "equal Justice," by using elections and "treating" the voters.

Extract from a letter from Newburn, N.C. July 26.

"The negroes in this town and neighbourhood have stirred a rumour of their having in contemplation to rise against their masters, and to procure themselves their liberty, the inhabitants have been alarmed and they keep a strict watch to prevent their gathering by numbers, and to prevent their procuring arms; should it become serious, which I don't think, the worst that could befal us would be if they should set the town on fire. — It is very absurd of the blacks, to suppose they could accomplish their views; and from the precautions that are taken to guard against a surprize, little danger is to be apprehended."

Pennsylvania Gazette (Philadelphia), August 15, 1792.

State of North Carolina Bertie County.

At a called Court begun and held on the 31st. day of May 1798 agreeable to Act of Assembly extending the right of trial of Slaves by a Jury – present the worshippfull William Cherry, David Turner, Benjamin Williams, and Aaron Spivey Esquires Justices — The following negroes to wit Duke a negro man the property of <*Jeremiah Freeman*> David Askew, Cuff a negroe man the property of Jeremiah Freeman, and Arthur a negroe man the property of the Orphans of Benjamin Wynns decd. where charged as follows (to wit) On the night of the 19th day of May in the year aforesaid, with several other negroes of said State, with force and arms, in the County aforesaid to wit, with Guns, clubs, swords, and knives, unlawfully did assemble and meet, and being as aforesaid Assembled and met, they the said negroes with divers other negroes, to the amount of one hundred and fifty, did in a violent and rebellious manner act and proceed, using and expressing words and actions indicative of a felonious attempt and wish and desire to overturn the law and police of the state aforesaid, and with malice aforethought, to murder and destroy the free white Inhabitants of said State. [. . .]

Trial of three blacks, May 31, 1798, Bertie County, Miscellaneous Records, Slave Records, State Archives, Office of Archives and History, Raleigh.

Extract of a letter from Wilmington, NC, dated July 5.

"For some weeks past a number of run away Negroes, who, in the day time secrete themselves in the swamps and woods in the vicinity of this town, have at night committed various depredations on the neighbouring plantations; not contented with these predatory excursions, they have added to their other enormities the murder of Mr. Jacob Lewis, overseer to A. D. Moore, Esq; and have also wounded Mr. Wm. Steely. — These continued outrages induced the Magistracy to outlaw the whole of the banditti, in consequence of which a number of them have been shot at different times and places; among the number killed is their chieftain, who stiled himself the General of the Swamps. And yesterday the following, who murdered Mr. Lewis, expiated his crimes by a public execution at Gallows Green. He confessed the crime, and acknowledged the justice of his sentence."

Pennsylvania Gazette (Philadelphia), July 29, 1795.

The examination of James a Negro Slave the property of the Widow Taylor taken before me at the House of Mr. Thomas Mutter of the County of Granville, on the 19th day of April 1794.

The said James saith that sometime about the Month of October or November last he was in company with Quillo, a negro Slave the property of James Hunt, when the said Quillo told him that he intended to give a treat to the black people at Craggs branch, where he intended to hold an election for the purpose of choosing Burgesses, Justices and Sheriffs, in order to have equal Justice distributed so that a weak person might collect his debt, as well as a Strong one, and that said Quillo advised him to stand as a Candidate (which he refused) that said Quillo told him he had a Barrel of Cydar and some Brandy with which he intended to treat and that if he, said James would do nothing else, he might sit down and drink, and that he intended to apply to Col. Smith and W. Young for have to hold said Election. Taken before me the day and year above mentioned.

M. Hunt J.P.

Trial of Quillo, 1794, Granville County, Miscellaneous Records, Miscellaneous Records of Slaves and Free Persons of Color, State Archives, Office of Archives and History, Raleigh.

Discipline and Punishment

Andrew's impending trial illustrates one tier of a bifurcated system of discipline to which slaves in North Carolina were subject: public courts, described below, and private "plantation justice." Plantation justice allowed slave owners to correct and chastise their bondsmen for petty offenses, theft of property belonging to masters, and most black-on-black crimes. According to John Brickell, such punishments might range from the forced consumption of tobacco worms to whipping. In the case of the latter, a slave might be compelled to administer the lashing, and others might be brought to the scene, all to impress the witnesses with the severity of the retribution in hopes of deterring such behavior in the future.

Whereas Mr. John Burnby hath given in upon Oath that he goes in Danger of his Life for feare of one Andrew a Negroe belonging to Mr. John Culpeper It is Ordered that Mr. Jno. Culpeper take Care of him and bring him to the next Court And alsoe give in good bond for his good behaviour to the next Court.

General Court, December 1684, in Mattie Erma Edwards Parker, ed., *North Carolina Higher-Court Records, 1670-1696*, Volume II of *The Colonial Records of North Carolina* [*Second Series*], ed. Mattie Erma Edwards Parker, William S. Price Jr., and Robert J. Cain (Raleigh: Division of Archives and History, Department of Cultural Resources [projected multivolume series, 1963-], 1968), 353.

The *Tobacco-worm;* I am not certain whether it is call'd by any other Name, but I have call'd it so from its feeding on the Tobacco-Leaves, it is exactly shaped like the *Galley-worm*, but is something larger, and not hairy, and has two sharp horns on its Head, the Body is white and Black, with as many Feet as the former. This Insect I take to be another Species of the *Scolopenders* and is destructive and pernicious in the *Tobacco* Plantations, if there be not care taken to Search for and kill them, which is a business that the Negroes are very much employed in during the Tobacco Season. I don't find that they are any way Poysonous, for I have known some of the Planters make their Negroes eat them by way of punishment, when they have been negligent in their Tobacco Fields, and have not carefully gathered them from amongst the Tobacco Leaves: [. . .]

John Brickell, *The Natural History of North Carolina* (1737; reprint, Murfreesboro, N.C.: Johnson Publishing Co., 1968), 168.

There are several Laws made against them in this Province to keep them in Subjection, and particularly one, *viz.*, That if a *Negroe* cut or wound his Master or a Christian with any unlawful Weapon, such as a *Sword, Scymiter,* or even a *Knife*, and there is a Blood-shed, if it is known amongst the Planters, they immediately meet and order him to be hanged, which is always performed by another *Negroe*, and generally the Planters bring most of their *Negroes* with them to behold their fellow *Negroe* suffer, to deter them from the like vile Practice. [. . .]

Brickell, *Natural History of North Carolina*, 272-273.

For capital offenses, North Carolina followed and refined Virginia legislation of 1692 and 1705 that tried slaves, accused of criminal actions, in special ad hoc courts. In North Carolina, the courts consisted of justices of the peace and slave-owning freeholders who possessed plenary powers as they arbitrarily heard evidence, made decisions, and meted out punishments when necessary. In most instances, the courts found the defendants guilty; occasionally they rendered a verdict of not guilty.

ACT III.

An act for the more speedy prosecution of slaves committing Capitall Crimes. [. . .]

Be it therefore enacted by their Majesties Lieutenant Governour, Councell and Burgesses of this present Generall Assembly and the authority thereof, and it is hereby enacted, That every negro or other slave which shall after this present session of Assembly commit or perpetrate any cappitall offence which the law of England requires to be satisfyed with the death of the offender or loss of member, after his commiting of the said offence, shall be forthwith committed to the common gaol of the county within which (*a*) such offence shall be committed, there to be safely continued, well laden with irons, and that the sheriff of the said county doe forthwith signifie the same to the governour for the time being, who is desired and impowered to issue out a commission of *oyer* and *terminer* directed to such persons of the said county as he shall think fitt, which persons forthwith after the receipt of the said commission are required and commanded publicly at the courthouse of the said county to cause the offender to be arraigned and indicted, and to take for evidence the confession of the party or the oaths of two witnesses or of one with pregnant circumstances, without the sollemnitie of jury, and the offender being found guilty as aforesaid, to pass judgment as the law of England provides in the like case, and on such judgment to award execution.

Laws, 1692, in William Waller Hening, ed., *The Statutes at Large; Being a Collection of All the Laws of Virginia*, 13 vols., 2d ed. (Philadelphia: the editor, by Thomas Desilver, 1820-1823), III:102-103.

CHAPTER XLVI.

An Act Concerning Servants & Slaves. [. . .]

XI. And Be It Further Enacted by the Authority afors'd that where any slave shall be guilty of any Crime or Offence whatsoever the same shall be heard & determined by any three Justices of the Precinct Court where such Offence or Crime shall be Committed & three Freeholders such as have Slaves in that Precinct or the Major part of them shall have full power & authority & they are hereby required & commanded to Trye the same according to their best Judgment & Discretion at such time & place as the first in Commission in the said precinct shall appoint & to pass Judgment for life or Member or any other Corporal Punishment on such Offender & cause Execution of the same Judgment to be made & done. [. . .]

Laws of North Carolina, 1715, in Walter Clark, ed., *The State Records of North Carolina*, 16 vols. (11-26) (Raleigh: State of North Carolina, 1895-1906), XXIII:62, 64.

North Carolina Hyde County ss. To any Lawfull Officer to Execute and make Returne.

Capt. Appleton Complains to me a Justice of the Peace for Said County that on the Twelvth Day of January 1772 – that a Negro Fellow named Oxford and a Negro Wench Named Jane Did Brake open the

Store House of Said Appleton and there did Steal take and Carry away Goods of a Considerable Value the property of the aforsaid Appleton.

There Fore I Command you in his Majestys Name to take Body of Said Negros Oxford and Jane that is the property of Rotheas Latham Esqrs. and them Safe keep so that you have them before me or Some other Justice of Said County to Answer the above Complaint Given under my hand and Seal this 14th Day of Janry 1772.

Saml. Smith

To the Sheriff of Hyd County you are hereby <*seal*> Commanded to take the Bodys of the within oxford and Jane and then Convey and Close Confine in the Common Goal at Woodstock untill there Shall be Special Court Called and held at said Woodstock for the further Tryal of the Said Negros Given under my hand and Seal this 14th Day of Janry. 1772.

Saml. Smith

North Carolina Hyde County ss. At a Special Court Called this 22d Day of January in the year of our Lord one thousand Seven hundrd Seventy Two. Present Edward McSwain, Saml. Smith, and Thomas Jones <*Esqrs. Justices*> Littleton Wilkins, Zachary Barrow, Benjn. Martin, and John Webster <*freeholders slave*>.

To try Certain Negros Slaves Called Oxford and Jane the Property of Rotheas Latham Esqr. for Feloniously Braking a Store house open and Steeling thereout Sundry Goods the Property of Benjamin Appleton who prosecutes.

Mr. Appleton being Sworne and Says upon his Oath on Sundy the 12th of this Month abought 4 Clock Left his Store about Seven Clock Came to the Store it was Broke open a Piece of Lining Gon and other things, Oxford Lying under the fence he went Called he was Saen with Goods under his Arm said Appleton pursued him Down to Mr. Lathams he Puled a Piece Linen from under his Arme Jane Produces Two Remnants of the Linen and Pipes found the Lock of the Store Broke and the Staple Drawn and found in the Middle of the floor Two Remnants of the Linen and four Knives was found and Delivered Said appleton by Rotheas Latham Esqr. a Peice of 25 yds. Stolen.

Rotheas Latham Esqr. Says on oath. Oxford had under his arme a Remnant of Linen he Said he Bought it of Mr. Parmarlee and on Search in Negro House found a Bottle Rum and thinks it was Sum of Appletons Rum Jane Says thought She Could find Some of the things Stole Jane Said She would not go with me Jain goes and Shoes and Remnant and 4 knives under the fence on going with a Light finds 5 Moore in the Kitchen Jane Said I Did Carry a Remnant of the Linnen and Put it into the shnegs of an appletree and said She found it.

Rebeccah Forman Says on Oath met the fellow Oxford on the Road and Dont not know of his having any thing perticular with him. Negro Man Holland the Property of Mrs. Cording on Examination Says he Saw Jane have four Knives in the Kitchen Comes and Covered them. Zack Caleb fourmans Negro Says he See Oxford Soling Down and See Jane Deliver to Oxford som Linin Mr. Appleton Declairs upon his Oath that the Linen and articules he found Part of was the Same he missed out of his Store and were his Property. Oxford upon his Examination Confessed he did take the Goods out of the Store and that no one was with him. Jan Confesed she found the knives on Oxfords Lodging and [moveed] them out for fear of her being Blaimd.

The Court Vallued the Said Negro man oxford to be Worth Seventy pound proclamation Money and the Negroe Woman Jane to be Worth forty pounds proc. money.

Whereupon the Court finds the Said oxford Guilty and awards Execution that he be Hanged by the neck untill He is Dead and be Executed by the Sheriff tomorrow at Two o clock in the after noon. And the Said Jane to have thirty Lashes well laid on her Bar Back to be Executed by the Sheriff imediately. Signed by

> Edward Mac Swain, Saml. Smith, and Thos. Jones <*Esqrs.*>, Littelton Wilkins, Zachy. Barrow, John Webster, and Benjn. Martin <*freeholders*>

Test
George Barrow Clk.

Trial of Oxford and Jane, Minutes of the Hyde County Court of Pleas and Quarter Sessions, January 12, 1772, State Archives, Office of Archives and History, Raleigh.

North Carolina Hyde County ss. At a Special Court held at Woodstock on thursday the fifth Day of June Anno Domini 1772. For the Tryal of a Negro Fellow Named Peeter the Property of Samuel Smith Esqr. for a Supposed felloney by him Said to be Committed. Present Edward Macswain, John Webster, Benjamin Hollowell <*Esquires Justices*>, Rotheas Latham, William Campbell, Major Clark, Thomas Gaylord <*Freeholder Masters of Slaves*>

The Court proceeded to Valuation and the Said Peter to be Worth Eighty pounds Proclamation Money.

The Charge of Complaint against the Negroe Peter is for Braking open the Store of Joseph Hancock in Woodstock and Stealing out of Said Store Dollars Gold and Paper Currency.

To which the Said Peter pleads Not Guilty.

And upon hearing the Several proofs offered against him and Maturely Considering the Same with every Circumstance the Court is of opinion that the Said Negroe Peter is not Guilty and therefore he is Discharged. Signed by

> Edward MacSwain (Seal), John Webster (Seal), Benjamin Hollowell (Seal) <*Esqrs. Justices*>, Rotheas Latham (Seal), Major Clark (Seal), Thomas Gaylord (Seal), William Campbell (Seal) <*Freeholders*>

Test. George Barrow Clk.

Trial of Peter, Minutes of the Hyde County Court of Pleas and Quarter Sessions, June 5, 1772, State Archives.

Punishment for felonious crimes varied according to the judgment of the courts. If offenses did not merit death, the courts generally ordered a whipping and the cropping of ears. For some thefts and such heinous crimes as rape, arson, poisoning, and murder the courts mandated execution, usually by hanging, but sometimes by burning at the stake. In some instances, the heads of those who had been hanged were severed and placed on posts as a reminder to other slaves of the consequences of their actions. Such vengeance might have explained the origin of the name of

the land at the confluence of the Northeast and Northwest Cape Fear Rivers at Wilmington—Negro Head Point.

Perquimans County. At a Special Court Begun and Opend and Held at Hertford in said County. Pursuant to a mittimus and summons Granted by William Wyatt Esqr. bearing date the 24th day of July and the 7th day of Augst 1759 and returned by the Sheriff of said County for the Tryall of a negro man named Ben Belonging to Mr. John Thach for Committing several Robberys and breaking [*torn*] Goal [...]

On hearing the Evidence and Considering the Offence the Court does direct the Sheriff forth with to have the said negro Ben to the whipping post and nail his right Ear to the Post and then [*torn*] him Remain for the spase of tenn minutes and then Cut off the one half of his Ear and give him fifty Lashes on his Bare Back well Laid on in the. In sentence of the Court and that the Sheriff deliver him to his Master or in his absence to his Mistress as soon as he Conveinently Cann. [...]

Trial of Ben, July 24, August 7, 1759, Perquimans County, Miscellaneous Records, Slave Records, Civil and Criminal Cases, State Archives, Office of Archives and History, Raleigh.

State of North Carolina Brunswick County. We the under named persons being Summoned as Justices of the Peace and freeholders of the County aforesaid to hold a court for the tryal of a Negro man Slave named Jamey the Property of Mrs. Sarah DuPré for the murder of Mr. Henry Williams of Lockwoods folly [...]

State of North Carolina Brunswick County. The Court proceeded on the tryal of the said Negro when he confessed himself to be one that had a hand in the murder of the said Henry Williams [...]

Ordered that the Sheriff take the said Jamey from hence to the place of Execution where he shall be tied to a Stake and Burnt alive.

Trial of Jamey, March 5, 1778, Slave Collection, State Archives, Office of Archives and History, Raleigh.

At a Court of Magistrates and Freeholders held at the Court House in Wilmington on Monday February 8th 1768 on the Tryal of a Negro Man named Quamino belonging to the Estate of John DuBois Esqr Deceased, charged with robbing sundry Persons—Present Cornelius

Harnett, John Lyon, Frederick Gregg, John Burgwin, and William Campbell <*Esqrs. Justices*> And John Walker, Anthony Ward, John Campbell, William Wilkinson <*Freeholders and Owners of Slaves*>.

The Court upon Examination of the Evidences relating to several Robberies committed by Quamino have found him guilty of the several Crimes charg'd against him, and Sentenced him to be hang'd by the Neck until he is dead to morrow morning between the hours of ten & twelve o'Clock and his head to be affixed up upon the Point near Wilmington.

William L. Saunders, ed., *The Colonial Records of North Carolina*, 10 vols. (Raleigh: State of North Carolina, 1886-1890), VII:685-686.

Slave owners suffered little economic hardship for their loss of property upon the execution of their slaves, because the government compensated them for the value of the bondsmen. However, the General Assembly decided in 1753 to disallow reimbursement if a slave owner had not properly fed and clothed a bondsman scheduled to be executed. The cost of compensation became so great that in 1758, during the French and Indian War, the General Assembly required the death penalty for male slaves only in cases of murder and rape, presumably in order to save money. The punishment for other felonies included castration, though that inhumane practice might cause death and consequent compensation. The legislation of 1758 was repealed in 1764 after the end of the war. Compensation for slave owners ended in 1787, though in 1796 the legislature reinstated that provision for seven counties.

CHAPTER XLVI.

An Act Concerning Servants & Slaves. [. . .]

XI. [. . .] And if any Slave shall be killed in apprehending or that shall by Judgment of the said Justices & Freeholders or the Major part of them be publickly executed to the Terror of other Slaves, such Justices & Freeholders shall give a Certificate of the Value of such Slave under their hands to the Master or Owner of such Slave who shall be thereby Entitulled to a Pole-Tax on all Slaves in the Government to make up that sum to the Owner of such Slave so publickly Executed or killed in Apprehending.

Laws, 1715, in Clark, *State Records*, XXIII:62, 64.

When any of these *Negroes* are put to death by the Laws of the Country, the Planters suffer little or nothing by it, for the Province is obliged to pay the full value they judge them worth to the Owner; this is the common Custom or Law in this Province, to prevent the Planters being ruined by the loss of their Slaves, whom they have purchased at so dear a rate; [. . .]

Brickell, *Natural History of North Carolina*, 273.

CHAPTER VI.

An additional Act to an Act concerning servants and slaves. [. . .]

IX. And be it further Enacted, by the authority aforesaid, That if any Slave or Slaves shall be killed on outlawry, or shall commit any Crime or Misdemeanor for which, he, she, or they, shall be capitally convicted, the Owner of such Slave or Slaves so outlawed or executed, shall be debarred all claim on the Public for the Value of such Slave or Slaves, and the Justices of the County Court and freeholders, who shall value the Slave or Slaves so killed, or sit on the Trial of such Slave or Slaves so capitally convicted, shall not make any certificate of the value of the same, unless it shall be made appear, on Motion for such Certificate, by the Owner, or some other Person, that such Slave or Slaves, killed on outlawry, or capitally convicted, shall have been sufficiently cloathed, and shall likewise have constantly received, for the preceding Year, an Allowance not less than a Quart of Corn per Diem.

Laws, 1753, in Clark, *State Records*, XXIII:388, 389-390.

CHAPTER VII.

An additional Act to an Act, intituled, An Act concerning Servants and Slaves. [. . .]

IV. And be it further Enacted, by the Authority aforesaid, That no male Slave shall for the First Offence, be condemned to Death, unless for Murder or Rape; but for every other Capital Crime, shall for the First Offence, suffer castration, which punishment every Court trying such Slave, shall be impowered, and are hereby directed to cause to, be inflicted; and the Sheriff shall cause such Judgment to be duly Executed; [. . .]

V. Provided always, That such Slave be valued by the Court Trying him, in the Usual Manner, that in case Death should ensue the Owner might be paid by the Public; [. . .]

Laws, 1758, in Clark, *State Records*, XXIII:488-489.

REPORT OF THE COMMITTEE OF PUBLIC CLAIMS, HELD AT WILMINGTON ON MONDAY, THE 26TH DAY OF APRIL, A.D. 1762. [. . .]

John Oliver was allowed thirty pounds, being the valuation money for a negro man called Tom, to him belonging, who was tried by the Special Court in Craven county and judgment that he should be castrated, which being put in execution, died by means of the operation in a short time after   £30 0 0

Clark, *State Records*, XXII:830.

CHAPTER XVII.

An Act to Repeal the Several Acts of Assembly Respecting Slaves Within This State, as far as the Same Relates to Making an Allowance to the Owner or Owners for any Executed or Outlawed Slave or Slaves.

Whereas many persons by cruel treatment to their slaves, cause them to commit crimes for which many of the said slaves are executed, whereby a very burdensome debt is unjustly imposed on the good citizens of this State:

For remedy whereof,

I. Be it Enacted by the General Assembly of the State of North Carolina, and it is Enacted by the authority of the same, That from and after the passing of this Act, the several Acts of Assembly of this State, as far as relates to making an allowance for any outlawed or executed slave or slaves, shall be, and the same is hereby repealed and made utterly void. (Passed Jan. 6, 1787).

Laws, 1787, in Clark, *State Records*, XXIV:809.

CHAP. XXVII.

An Act *making compensation to the owners of outlawed and executed slaves, for the counties of Bladen, Halifax, Granville, Cumberland, Perquimans, Beaufort and Pitt.*

I. BE *it enacted by the General Assembly of the state of North-Carolina, and it is hereby enacted by the authority of the same,* That when a slave shall be tried in any of the counties aforesaid, and shall be found guilty by the jury of any crime, the punishment whereof shall extend to life, the said jury shall fix and ascertain the value of the said slave, and shall give the said valuation in at the time they return their verdict; which said valuation shall be certified by the chairman of the court and given to the owner of the said slave, who shall be entitled to receive two thirds of such valuation from the Sheriff of any of the said counties in which such slave may have been executed.

Laws of the State of North-Carolina, 1796, c. 27.

Slaves possessed no legal protection from the summary justice administered by masters and courts until the eve of the Revolution. In 1771, Martin Howard, chief justice of the colony, delivered a sensational charge to the grand jury of the North Carolina Superior Court. A slaveholder reared in Rhode Island, Howard in his charge questioned the morality, if not the very legitimacy, of slavery. He pointed out to incipient American revolutionaries that while they sought to protect their rights from the intrusion of Britain, they literally denied the natural right of freedom to their slaves over whom they wielded the power of life and death.

WILMINGTON, (North-Carolina) *Feb.* 12

From the CAPE FEAR MERCURY.

Part of a charge delivered to the Grand Jury, at a late Superior Court, by the Honorable Martin Howard, Esq;

I Will beg your further attention, gentlemen, to a few observations, which I am led to make from a circumstance which happened at a late superior court.

A white man was indicted for the murder of a negro slave, and the grand jury returned the Bill IGNORAMUS. I cannot pretend to know their reasons for doing so; it might possibly be owing to want of sufficient evidence of the fact; but I am rather inclined to believe they founded their opinion upon this principle; THAT IT IS NOT MURDER FOR A WHITE MAN TO KILL A NEGRO SLAVE.

Such a principle as this, I take to be of a most pernicious nature, tending to a gross corruption both of the understanding, and the heart, and at the same time repugnant to law. [. . .]

But be this as it may, it must be confessed that in the plantations the lawfulness of slavery is generally admitted. Great part of the property here consists in negroes — and that sort of policy which avarice and luxury have made necessary, and which sacrifices justice and humanity to the acquisition of wealth, and the enlargement of commerce, has given a sanction to slavery, and incorporated it with our laws.

Nevertheless, I am not alone in my opinion, that slavery is not only in itself a great evil, but produces the worst effect upon our manners. — Accustomed to an uncontrolable power over slaves, men become lazy, proud, and cruel; and we may reasonably conclude that these vices, so hurtful to ourselves and to society, would become still more enormous if we should adopt so barbarous a maxim as, that a white man may murder a slave with impunity. [. . .]

What apology or answer could we make to a negro slave, who should remonstrate and say to us, "You invoke Heaven and earth against a claim to take from you a trifling sum of money without your consent, or to try you without a jury, when you are charged with any crime; and are you so judicially hardened and reprobate as to take from us every right and privilege of humanity?" The reproof would be just, and it is not easy to express one's indignation to behold men, with an unfeeling indifference, holding their fellow creatures in the most miserable bondage; but when they imagine their own liberty is in the least invaded, they will gravely, and without blushing, quote every writer upon government and civil society to prove, that all men are by nature equal and by nature free. [. . .]

Slavery is an adventitious, not a natural state. The souls and bodies of negroes are of the same quality with ours — they are our own fellow creatures, tho' in humbler circumstances, and are capable of the same happiness and misery with us.

Excepting the fruits of his labour, which belong to the master, a slave retains all the rights of subjects under civil government that are NATURALLY UNALIENABLE: Of this kind is self-defence, and personal safety from violence. No one has a right to take away his life without being punished for it. No civil law can confer such a right; it would confound every principle of nature.

But to show that the notion here opposed is contrary to law, as well as to reason, I shall conclude in giving you the definition of murder, as it is laid down in all the books.

"Murder is, when a man of sound mind and memory, and of the age of discretion, unlawfully killeth any REASONABLE CREATURE, being under the king's peace." So that if we can persuade ourselves, that a negro slave is a reasonable creature, it must be murder in any one that shall feloniously slay him.

I am content it should be said, that these observations proceed more from the heart than the understanding, at the same time I shall ever suspect the soundness of that understanding which has no mixture of humanity.

Don Higginbotham and William S. Price Jr., "Was It Murder for a White Man to Kill a Slave? Chief Justice Martin Howard Condemns the Peculiar Institution in North Carolina," *William and Mary Quarterly*, 3d ser., 36 (October 1979): 597-598, 599, 601.

Howard's moving testimonial may have led to North Carolina's first attempt to provide slaves with some relief from arbitrary treatment by whites. Legislation in 1774 made the killing of a slave punishable by law, albeit with broad exceptions. Influenced perhaps by the successful outcome of the Revolution and by the increasing sympathy for the plight of bondsmen by various religious denominations, particularly the Quakers, the legislature in 1791 amended the 1774 law to make killing a slave a capital offense upon the first conviction, though again with exceptions. In 1793 the General Assembly accorded bondsmen the protection

of a jury trial in capital cases. **Trials proceeded as formerly, with the exception of the inclusion of jurors; the outcomes apparently were little changed.**

CHAPTER XXXI.

An Act to Prevent the wilful and malicious killing of Slaves.

Whereas some Doubts have arisen with Respect to the Punishment proper to be inflicted upon such as have been guilty of willfully and maliciously killing Slaves:

I. Be it therefore Enacted by the Governor, Council, and Assembly, and by the Authority of the same, That from and after the first day of May next, if any Person shall be guilty of wilfully and maliciously killing a Slave, so that, if he had in the same Manner killed a Freeman, he would by the Laws of the Realm be held and deemed guilty of Murder, that then and in that Case such Offender shall, upon due and legal Conviction thereof, in the Superior Court of the District where such offence shall happen, or have been committed, suffer twelve Months Imprisonment: And upon a second Conviction thereof, shall be adjudged guilty of Murder, and shall suffer Death, without benefit of Clergy.

II. And be it further Enacted by the Authority aforesaid, That if the Slave so wilfully and maliciously killed, shall be the property of another, and not of the Offender, he shall on the first Conviction thereof, pay the Owner thereof such sum as shall be the Value of the said Slave, to be assessed by the Inferior Court of the County where such Slave was killed, and shall stand committed to the Gaol of the District where such conviction shall happen, until he shall satisfy and pay the said Sum so assessed.

III. Provided always, That this Act shall not extend to any Person killing any Slave outlawed by virtue of any Act of Assembly in this Province, or to any Slave in the Act of Resistance to his lawful Owner or Master, or to any Slave dying under moderate Correction.

Laws, 1774, in Clark, *State Records*, XXIII:975-976.

CHAP. IV.

An Act *to amend an Act, entitled,* An Act to prevent thefts and Robberies by Slaves, free Negroes and Mulattoes, *passed at Tarborough in the Year one thousand seven hundred and eighty-seven; and to amend an Act, passed in the Year one thousand seven hundred and seventy-four, entitled,* An Act to prevent the wilful and malicious killing of slaves. [. . .]

III. And whereas by another act of Assembly passed in the year 1774 the killing a slave however wanton, cruel and deliberate, is only punishable in the first instance by imprisonment and paying the value thereof to the owner; which distinction of criminality between the murder of a white person and of one who is equally an human creature, but merely of a different complexion, is disgraceful to humanity and degrading in the highest degree to the laws and principles of a free, christian and enlightened country : *Be it enacted by the authority aforesaid* That if any person shall hereafter be guilty of wilfully and maliciously killing a slave such offender shall upon the first conviction thereof be adjudged guilty of murder, and shall suffer the same punishment as if he had killed a free man; any law, usage or custom to the contrary notwithstanding. *Provided always,* That this act shall not extend to any person killing a slave outlawed by virtue of any act of Assembly of this state, or to any slave in the act of resistance to his lawful owner or master, or to any slave dying under moderate correction.

Laws, 1791, c. 4.

CHAP. V.

An Act to extend the right of trial by jury to slaves.

BE *it enacted by the General Assembly of the state of* North-Carolina, *and it is hereby enacted by the authority of the same,* That in all cases hereafter happening, where any slave shall be accused of an offence, the punishment whereof shall extend to life, limb, or member, such slave shall be entitled to trial by jury, on oath, consisting of twelve good and lawful men, owners of slaves, in a summary way, and in open Court of the county wherein such offence was committed. *Provided nevertheless,* That if the Court of the county shall not meet within fifteen days from the time of commitment, the Sheriff of the county shall and may summon three Justices of the Peace of the said county, and a jury of good and lawful men owners of slaves, who shall have as full and ample power and authority to try and pass sentence on any slave accused and brought to trial before them, as the County Court might or could have by virtue of this act. *And provided always*, That the said jury and three Justices shall not be connected with the owner of such slave, or the prosecutor, either by affinity or consanguinity. [. . .]

Laws, 1793, c. 5.

State of North Carolina Onslow County. at a Court begun and held for The County of Onslow at the Court House In Onslow on the 2nd day of August in the year of our lord one Thousand eight Hundred and in the 25 year of American Independance for the Tryal of a Negro Slave the property of Edwd. Dudley dec. Charged with breaking open and entering the house of John Corber and feloniously Robing and taking out of the house and carrying of One New Shirt One drest deerskin one new wallet Sixteen hens eggs Some tobacco one tickler bottle the whole amounting to three pounds of the goods and Chattels of the Said Corbit.

Present the Worshipful James Foy, Daniel Shepard and Benjn. Oliver Esquires. Defendant pleads not Guilty.

The following Juryors were returned and sworn

1. Richd. Ward	4. Edwd. Hammond
2. Isaa Charles Craft	5. James Thompson
3. John Farr	6. Wm. Norman
7. Joseph Mashborn	10. Richd. King
8. Thomas Mashborn	10. Owen Jones
9. Drura Dunn	12. Benjn. Bryan.

The following witness Came forward and was sworn.

Jno. Corbit Prosecutor, [Sadit] Greear and Dave a Negro the property of James Foy Esqr. after which under a Charge of the Court the Jury retired but soon after returned With the following verdict Guilty.

The negro march Condemnd to death was Valued by the said Jury at 275 dollars.

The Court then proceeded to pass Sentence that the prisinor March is guilty of death and to be Executed and hanged on tuesday next at the

Common place of Execution Given under Our hands and Seals this 2nd day Augt. 1800.

> D. Shepard C,
> Benjn. Oliver JP.
> Jas. Foy j.p

Test Nath. Loomiss cc

Trial of March, August 2, 1800, Onslow County, Miscellaneous Records, Slave (Criminal Actions Concerning), State Archives, Office of Archives and History, Raleigh.

At a Court Called and held at the Court House in Edenton on the 30th day of January in the year 1797 for the Trial of Negroe Girl Bett the property of Doctor Samuel Dickinson Esquire, being Charged with Setting Fire to the Dwelling House of said Samuel Dickinson. Present the worshippfull William Borritz, John Marr, Jacob Blount, William Littlejohn <Esquires Justices>. 1. Alexander Millen, 2. Charles Laughree, 3. Samuel Butler, 4. Lemuel Standin, 5. Thomas Harkins, 6. John Little, 7. King Druton, 8. James Neill, 9. Thomas Saterfield, 10. James Granberry, 11. John Horniblow, 12. Honeas Neil.

The prisoner Negroe Bett being Charged Plead not Guilty.

The above Jury being Impanelled and Sworn on this Trial Say the prisoner is Not Guilty.

Trial of Bett, January 30, 1797, Chowan County, Miscellaneous Records, Slave Records, State Archives, Office of Archives and History, Raleigh.

As they became more and more numerous, and in the estimation of whites, more threatening, slaves not only endured trial by the special courts, but they also faced the search or patrol. The neighboring colonies of South Carolina and Virginia instituted the patrol system in 1704 and 1727, respectively; the North Carolina legislature established it by law in 1753, doubtless in reaction to a reported slave uprising in the Lower Cape Fear. Accordingly, searchers or patrollers were required periodically to inspect slave habitations for weapons and to apprehend slaves who did not carry proper passes or identification. After independence the General Assembly, in 1779, continued the patrol; in 1794, it required patrollers to search their districts

biweekly rather than monthly, an indication presumably of the increasing threat posed by bondsmen.

No. 233. *AN ACT* TO SETTLE A PATROLL.

WHEREAS on the sight or advice of an enemy it will be necessary for the safety and defence of the inhabitants of this Collony to draw together to the sea coast, or such other place as the Generall shall direct, all the forces thereof; to prevent such insurrections and mischiefs as from the great number of slaves we have reason to suspect may happen when the greater part of the inhabitants are drawn together,

I. *Be it enacted* by his Excellency John Lord Granville, Palatine, and the rest of the true and absolute Lords and Proprietors of this Province, by and with the advice and consent of the rest of the members of the General Assembly, now met at Charlestown for the south-west part of this Province, That the Generall do nominate and commissionate one or more captains or officers in every company, and the Generall is requested to appoint one or more captains or officers as aforesaid, and give him or them power to enlist under their respective commands ten men of every company which shall be nominated by the Generall, which men so enlisted shall be discharged of the service of that captain or officer of that company they did before belong to, and shall serve under that captain or officer to be appointed as aforesaid; and every person so enlisted shall provide for himselfe and allwayes keep a good horse, a case of pistolls and a carbine, or other gunn, a sword, a cartouch box, with at least twelve cartridges in it, under the penalty of tenn shillings for want of any one or more things as aforesaid, and shall appear accoutred as aforesaid as often as the captain or officer shall command him to do so, at such time and place as he shall appoint, or forfeit for every neglect of appearance on ordinary occasions, the sume of ten shillings, and for every neglect of appearance in time of allarm the sume of ten pounds, and shall be on all occasions obedient to and behave himselfe towards his respective captain or officer, as by an Act entituled an Act for the Better Settleing and Regulateing the Militia and appointing Look-Outs, every soldier is obliged to, under the paines and forfeitures in the said Act appointed.

Laws, 1704, in Thomas Cooper, ed., *The Statutes at Large of South Carolina*, 22 vols. ed. Thomas Cooper, David J. McCord, and successive secretaries of state (Columbia, S.C.: A. S. Johnston, 1836-1898), II:254.

CHAPTER VI.

An additional Act to an Act concerning servants and slaves. [. . .]

IV. And be it further Enacted, That the Justices of each County Court, when and where they judge it necessary, shall divide their respective Counties into Districts, and yearly, at the first Court to be held for their Counties respectively after the first day of May, shall appoint three Freeholders in each District as Searchers, who shall take the following Oath, viz.:

I, A. B., do swear that I will, as Searcher for Guns, Swords, and other Weapons, among the Slaves in my District faithfully, and as privately as I can, discharge the Trust reposed in me, as the Law directs, to the best of my power. So help me God.

Which Searchers shall four Times in a Year or oftener if they think necessary, search and examine the Quarters and the other Places where Negroes resort in their District, for any Gun, Sword, or other Weapon, and upon finding any of the said Weapons, are hereby required to seize the same, and convert them to their own use, as by the afore-recited Act is directed.

V. And be it further Enacted, That any Person appointed Searcher as aforesaid, who shall neglect or refuse to act, shall forfeit and pay the Sum of Forty Shillings, Proclamation Money, to such Person, who shall next succeed him; to be recovered as other Fines in this Act mentioned.

VI. And for the Encouragement of such Searchers faithfully to execute their Office, Be it further Enacted, by the authority aforesaid, That each and every Searcher shall, as to his own Person, be, during the Time of his Continuance in his Office, exempted from serving as a Constable, or upon the Roads, or in the Militia, or as a Juror, and shall not be obliged to pay any Provincial, County, or Parish Tax, of what Kind or Nature soever.

Laws, 1753, in Clark, *State Records*, XXIII:388-389.

CHAPTER VII.

An Act to amend an Act, entitled, An Additional Act concerning Servants and Slaves, passed at New Bern in the year One Thousand Seven hundred and fifty three, and other purposes therein mentioned.

I. Whereas by the before recited act, the encouragement given to searchers or patrollers, the penalty inflicted on them in case of a non compliance of their duty, and the times appointed for searching, are insufficient;

II. Be it therefore enacted by the General Assembly of the State of North Carolina, and it is hereby enacted by the authority of the same, that each and every searcher or patroller appointed in pursuance of the aforesaid act shall, as to his own person, during the time of his continuance in office, be exempted from serving as a constable, or working upon the roads, attending private musters, or as a juror, and shall be entitled to such further allowance out of the county tax as the court shall think necessary.

III. And be it further enacted by the authority aforesaid, that the searchers in their respective districts shall search once in every month for guns and other weapons, as the before recited act directs, and shall make return on oath of all such guns, or other weapons, which they shall so find, to the succeeding county court, to be applied to the use of the county, or returned to the owner, as the court may direct; and in case they find any slave or slaves on the Sabbath, or other unseasonable time, off his master or mistress's plantation, without a pass, or in company with some white person who will vouch for his or their honest intention, it shall be lawful for them to apprehend such slave or slaves, and convey, or cause to be conveyed, to the master, mistress, or overseer, who shall pay to the said searchers or patrollers in like manner as for apprehending and conveying runaways, as a compensation for their trouble.

Laws, 1779, in Clark, *State Records*, XXIV:276.

CHAP. IV.

An Act *to prevent the owners of slaves from hiring to them their time, to make compensation to Patrolls, and to restrain the abuses committed by free negroes and mulattoes.* [. . .]

III. *And be it further enacted,* That the Justices of the courts of pleas and quarter-sessions, if they deem it necessary, shall at the first or second court which shall be held after the first day of January, in the year one thousand [s]even hundred and ninety-five; and the first court which shall be held after the first day of January in each year afterwards, appoint in each Captain's district or company, any number, not exceeding six discreet and proper persons, to act as Patrollers for the space of one year; and as a compensation for the services required of them as such, shall be exempted from serving on juries, working on roads, and from the payment of all county and parish taxes to the amount of forty shillings, and in addition to the fees hitherto allowed by law, the Patrollers so appointed shall be entitled to receive the one half of the penalties recovered under this act in the district in which such Patrollers may respectively act and reside, except such penalties as may be incurred by hiring to negroes their own time.

IV. *And be it further enacted,* That it shall be the duty of the Patrollers, or two of them at least, appointed as aforesaid, to patrol their respective districts once at least in two weeks, for the purpose of carrying this act into effect; and on failure or neglect to perform such services, every person so failing or neglecting shall forfeit and pay the sum of ten pounds, recoverable before any jurisdiction having cognizance thereof, one half to the use of the informer, and the other half to the use of the county where the same is recoverable.

Laws, 1794, c. 4.

Most counties in the eastern and central sections of the colony, wherein resided the majority of slaves, availed themselves of the patrol law of 1753. The paucity of slaves in the west rendered patrollers unnecessary in such counties as Orange and Tryon, while the justices of the Craven County court, in eastern North Carolina, immediately appointed them. The Granville County court issued explicit instructions to its patrollers, requiring oaths of office, explaining their duties, and defining a "lawful pass" and "unlawful assembly" for the benefit of the searchers.

<6 month> Ordered that George Johnston and Matthew Arthur be Appointed patrolers within the Town of Newbern.

<6 month> Charles Rew and John Lovett from Handcocks *<Clubfoots>* Creek to the Bound of the County Downwards.

William Smith and Bengjah Daly from Handcocks Creek to Mill *<Island>* Creek.

Edward Franck and Adam Moore from NewBern Town to Higgins Bridge.

Samuel Fealds and John Jones from Higgins Bridge Including Chinkapin and so to the Southwest Bridge.

William Barron Samuel Pope and William Wiggins from So.West to NewBern.

<6 mo.> William Mixon in the fork of Swifts Creek and Nuce River so up to the Head of the County.

<6 month> Jacob Johnson and William Garrold from the Head Swifts Creek on the No. side to Hills Creek.

<6 mo.> William Spight and Cason Brinson Junr. from Hills Creek to Bear Creek.

<6 month> John Franckling and James Carraway from Beards Creek to Lower Broad Creak.

Minutes of the Craven County Court of Pleas and Quarter Sessions, November 1753, State Archives, Office of Archives and History, Raleigh.

To Carry into Effect an Act of the last General Assembly intitled an act, an act to impower the Several County Courts within this State to appoint patroles.

1st. It is ordered that it shall be the duty of the Justices of the Peace in this County, if they deem it necessary, or on application of two or more respectable freeholders within the District where his may reside, to proceed with advice of the Capt. of the District to appoint such number of patroles as he may deem necessary not Exceeding Six to serve any length of time he may think proper not Exceeding one Year *<Months>*, It shall farther be the duty of the Justices so appointing patroles to transmitt a list of them to the Clerk of the Court Whose duty it shall be to Enter them on his Records.

2nd. It shall be the duty of the Patroles so appointed to patrole there respective districts at least twice in every month <*two times*>.

3. There has arisan Many doubts in the minds of the Citizens of this County what is a lawfull pass also what is an unlawfull assembly, for remedy thereof it is ordered that no pass shall be deemed Suffecient unless it Specifies the time they are to pass and the place or places they are going to also it shall be deemed an unlawfull assembly if more than three are found togather even with such a pass as above Specified unless at the time they are going to or from Meeting or while there to hear a In[*blank*] this order is not to be construed so asto prevent Negroes from going to see thier wives Where they have intermarried by consent of there respective masters, no slave caught shall receive more than 15 lashes moderately laid on by the Patroles, but on Misbehavour carried before a Justice to be dealt with ast they law may directs.

4. It shall farther be the duty of Patroles so appointd to Search all Suspected Negroe Houses for all sorts of War like implements and if any such found they deliver them to some Justice of the peace in the district when, they belong whose duty is shall be to render a true account of all such articles as may be found and deposited to the Sucseeding Court held for the County to be dealt on as they Law <*Court*> may direct.

5. Before the patroles so appointed shall proceed, they shall take the following oath, you and Each of you shall Swear that you will faithfully and truly, to the best of your <*there*> ability carry the foregoing orders into Effect that you nor neither of you will through Malice or hatred either to the Master or slave, beat or abuse any slave caught by you, nor will you or Either of you through fear or affection favor any, but well and Truly deal out Justice to all to the best of your knowledge and Ability so help your god.

Instructions of the Granville County Court for appointing patrollers, n. d., Granville County, Miscellaneous Records, Miscellaneous Records of Slaves and Free Persons of Color, State Archives, Office of Archives and History, Raleigh.

The patrol system failed to satisfy fully its intended purpose as indicated by the legislation of 1779. Although the original law exempted searchers from jury and militia duty as well as from provincial, county, and parish taxes, patrollers proved negligent, resulting in individual dismissals or the suspension of the entire patrol in a county. Patrollers also encountered opposition from slave owners who disliked harsh treatment meted out to their bondsmen. Although masters had little recourse against abusive patrollers, legislation in 1794 required at least two searchers to be on duty at all times and limited punishment of slaves to fifteen lashes per offense. Sometimes their numbers proved inadequate to perform the task required of them, as was the case in Bertie County.

It is Ordered by the Court that the patroles be all Discharged for not doing their Duty.

Minutes of the Chowan County Court of Pleas and Quarter Sessions, July, October 1755, State Archives, Office of Archives and History, Raleigh.

September 26th 1785. To the Worshipfull Court now Sitting, May it please your Worships, We the Subscribers think Necessary as Well for the benefit of our Neighbours As our Selves, that their Should be Patroles appointed For keeping the Negroes in better Subjection although there is Patroles appointed Very few of them do their duty, by Which means there is Anumber of Negroes Passing and unpassing at all times of the Night Without Liberty from their Owners much to the Injury of our property, therefore We the Subscribers Humbly pray you'd Appoint us Patroles requesting no indulgence or Exemption for our Services.

Saml. Creecy, Fred Creecy, Richard Benbury, Nathan Creecy

Chowan County, Miscellaneous Records, Slave Records, State Archives.

Ordered that Court assummons issue for William Lewis Peter Loyman Samuell Poppleston, James Thompson to shew Cause etc. Concerning obstructing the Patrollers in their duty etc.

Minutes of the Chowan County Court of Pleas and Quarter Sessions, July 1758, State Archives.

CHAP. IV.

An Act to prevent the owners of slaves from hiring to them their time, to make compensation to Patrolls, and to restrain the abuses committed by free negroes and mulattoes. [. . .]

V. *And be it further enacted,* That the Patrollers in each district, or a majority of those present, shall have power to inflict a punishment, not exceeding fifteen lashes, on all slaves they may find off their owner's plantation, or travelling on the Sabbath, or other unseasonable time, without a proper permit or pass.

Laws, 1794, c. 4.

[. . .] And the state aforesaid charge that the said Negroes with other Negroes to the number aforesaid armed as aforesaid and in the county aforesaid did attack pursue knock down and lay prostrate the patrollers of said County in the lawful execution of their duty, [. . .]

Trial of three slaves, May 31, 1798, Bertie County, Miscellaneous Records, Slave Records, State Archives, Office of Archives and History, Raleigh.

———

At the beginning of the American Revolution, when rumors of slave insurrections abounded and the presence of the British military offered the possibility of freedom for bondsmen, the revolutionaries redoubled their efforts to suppress their slaves. Special patrols were created in counties such as New Hanover and Pitt. County committees of safety attempted to disarm slaves and gave patrols plenary authority to deal with recalcitrant blacks. Recognizing the limitations of the patrol, however, Craven County resorted to its militia to maintain order among the slaves. The General Assembly eventually recognized that patrols could not triumph over large numbers of armed slaves; therefore, in 1795 they directed county militia units to take action when necessary to meet such threats.

WEDNESDAY, [JUNE 21] 10 O'CLOCK.

The Committee met According to Adjournment. [. . .]

On Motion, for the more effectually disarming & keeping the Negroes in order within the County of New Hanover — It was Unanimously agreed by the Members of the Committee for said County to Appoint Patroles to search for & take from Negroes all kinds of Arms whatsoever, & such Guns or other Arms found with Negroes shall be delivered to the Captain of the Company of the District in which they are found, to be distributed by the Said Officers to those of his Company who may be in want of Arms & who are not able to purchase them, & that the following persons be Patrols as follows:

From Beaufords ferry to the End of Mr. Geo. Moore's District —

Sam'l Swann	Tho's Moseley	Geo. Palmer
Henry Beauford	Wm. Robeson	Luke Woodward

Burgaw —

Sampson Moseley	William Moseley	Jno. Ashe, Jr.

Black River —

Geo. Robeson	Tho's Devane	Jno. Colvin
Tho's Corbett, Jr.	Benj. Robeson	James Bloodworth

Welch Tract —

Barnaby Fuller	Geo. McGowan	Wm. Wright
Martin Wells	Morgan Swinney	David Jones

Leora H. McEachern and Isabel M. Williams, eds., *Wilmington-New Hanover Safety Committee Minutes, 1774-1776* (Wilmington, N.C.: Wilmington-New Hanover County American Revolution Bi-Centennial Association, 1974), 30.

Proceedings of the Safety Committee in Pitt County.

MARTINBOROUGH, Saturday, July 8th 1775.

The Committee of this County meat this Day and has resolved as under mentioned Viz:

Resolved, that the Patrolers [have power to] shoot one or any number of Negroes who are armed and doth not willingly surrender their arms, and that they have Discretionary Power, to shoot any Number of Negroes above four, who are off their Masters Plantations, and will not submitt. And the Damage that Owners of any Negro who shall be killed or Disabled in consequence of this Resolve to be paid by Poll Tax on all the Taxable Negroes in the County.

The Committee is adjourned till Monday week, July the 17th 1775.

JOHN SIMPSON, Chairman.

Saunders, *Colonial Records*, X:87.

Whereas the frequent assembling together of slaves and disorderly persons in this Critical and alarming time when the Enemies of American Liberty are using every means in their power to disswade the good people of this State from their Allegiance to the same may have a tendency to increase those disorders, Ordered that it be Recommended by this Court to the several Militia captains in the Regiment of Craven that they do as Soon as possible Direct such part of their Companys to Patrole in the different Neighbourhoods as often as Occasion may require, And if such Patroles should find any Negroe Slaves or other persons misbehaving themselves that they have Power to Inflict a Punishment on such offending Slaves not exceeding Ten Lashes, And if an offense of a higher nature to apprehend such disorderly persons or Slaves and Carry them before a Justice of the Peace to be Dealt with according to Law.

Minutes of the Craven County Court of Pleas and Quarter Sessions, September 1777, State Archives.

CHAP. XVI.

An Act *to prevent any person who may emigrate from any of the West-India or Bahama Islands, or the French, Dutch or Spanish settlements on the Southern coast of America, from bringing slaves into this state, and also for imposing certain restrictions on free persons of colour who may hereafter come into this state.* [. . .]

V. *And be it further enacted,* That when any number of negroes, or other slaves, or free people of colour, shall collect together in arms, and be going about the country, committing thefts and alarming the inhabitants of any county, it shall be the duty of the commanding officer of such county, or Captain of a troop of horse, upon three or more Justices of the Peace requiring the same, immediately to call out a sufficient number to suppress such depredations or insurrections; which detachment of militia shall be under the same rules and regulations, as in cases of invasion and insurrection, and shall be entitled to receive the same pay and rations as the troops of the United States, when in actual service; and if any person shall be wounded or disabled in suppressing such insurrection, he shall be provided for at the public expence, in the same manner as heretofore practiced in this state. [. . .]

Laws, 1795, c. 16.

Urban Slavery

Slaves inhabited the few urban centers in early North Carolina, particularly Wilmington, New Bern, and Edenton along the coast. They handled much of the domestic drudgery in the towns, manned shops, operated drays, and constructed houses and public buildings. In the coastal region, slaves figured prominently in maritime activities, serving as stevedores on the docks, pilots along the rivers, and cooks, stewards, and sailors on ships. Women worked in towns as cooks, laundresses, and house-keepers. Wilmington slaves helped to fight fires, repair the streets, and build the town's famed arches (later tunnels) for directing the flow of streams through the town.

At a meeting of the Commissioners for the Town of Wilmington on Tuesday 21st July 1778. [. . .]

[John] Gilliard proposed to work the Fire Engines & to find four able Negroes for that purpose, once a month, from the date hereof to the 21st Jany 1779, for the sum of Six pounds five shillings currency AGREED.

Also to cover the Brick Arch & raise the ground 15 feet each side from Mrs. Boyd's fence to Mr. Benning's and to repair & clean the Streets, he finding a good and sufficient Cart, with two horses & two able Negroes for that purpose, & that he will personally attend to see the said work accomplished, for the sum of Three pounds, 10/ per day.

[AGREED]

Donald R. Lennon and Ida B. Kellam, eds., *The Wilmington Town Book, 1743-1778* (Raleigh: Division of Archives and History, Department of Cultural Resources, 1973), 237.

At a meeting of the Commissioners for the Town of Wilmington on Tuesday the 15th Decr. 1778. [. . .]

ORDERED that the Clerk pay to Mrs. Priscilla Kennon the sum of Ten Pounds for Negro hire working on the Arch.

ORDERED that the Clerk pay to Frans. Brice the sum of Five pounds Eight shillings for negro hire work on the Arch.

Lennon and Kellam, *Wilmington Town Book*, 239.

In the towns, bondsmen enjoyed considerable freedom. Like the white population, they gathered in houses and thoroughfares, stayed out after dark, and sometimes rode horses recklessly through the streets. But such behavior among slaves disturbed and even intimidated whites, who responded by imposing curfews, establishing patrols, passing various restrictive ordinances, and punishing malefactors. These actions were largely ineffective.

At a meeting of the Commissioners of the Town of Wilmington on Monday the 19th day of September 1768. [. . .]

ORDERED that any Slave or Slaves that shall be found playing or making a noise in the Streets so as to Disturb any of the Inhabitants of this Town every slave so offending shall receive at the publick Whipping Post thirty lashes on his or her bare back, unless the owners of such slave or slaves shall pay to the Commissioners the sum of Five Shillings Proclamation money. [. . .]

Lennon and Kellam, *Wilmington Town Book*, 186, 187.

[. . .] That Absolam Taylor and Samuel Hughey act as patrolers for the Burrow of Salisbury.

Minutes of the Rowan County Court of Pleas and Quarter Sessions, May 1775, State Archives, Office of Archives and History, Raleigh.

At a meeting of the Commissioners for the Town of Wilmington of Tuesday the 18th August 1778. [. . .]

ORDERED that if any slave or slaves be found in the Streets of this Town after the hour of 9 oClock at night, from the 20th day of March to the 22nd day of September or after 10 oClock from the 23d day of September to the 19th day of March, or the ringing of the Bell at those hours of the night (unless such slave or slaves have a Ticket from their Master or Mistress, or have a Candle & Lanthorn) shall be taken up by any Inhabitant of this Town & put in the Stocks, and receive Thirty Nine lashes on their bare back at the Publick Whipping Post.

Lennon and Kellam, *Wilmington Town Book*, 238.

On Monday the Twenty nineth day of January in the year of our Lord one thousand Seven hundred and Sixty five. The Mayor, Alderman and Freeholders of the Borrough of Wilmington Convened in Common Council at the Court house therein.

Present—

The Worshipfull Frederick Gregg, Esquire, Mayor

Cornelius Harnett
John Lyon
John DuBois   Esquires, Aldermen
Samuel Green
Moses John DeRosset
William Campble

Together with the Freeholders, Vizt.—

John Corbin, Alexander Duncan, Archd. Maclaine, John Burgwin, Anthony Ward, William Wilkenson, James Moran, Malatia Hamilton, John Mortimer, Alexander Ross, William McKinzey, Benjamine Stone, Caleb Mason, Thomas Cunningham, David Brown, Magnus Cowan, Robert Wells, Robert McCracken, Richard Player, Stephen Player. [. . .]

And WHEREAS the Immodirate riding of Horses thro' the Streets of this Borrough may be attended with very bad and dangerous consequence.

Be it therefore Ordained by the authority aforesaid, That if any Negro or other Slave shall after the said tenth day of February next presume to ride any Horse, Mare or Guilding immoderately or uncommonly fast thro' or over any Street, Alley, passage, or other place within this Borrough, or run any Race or Races, with any Horse, Mare or Guilding along any Street or Vacant Lot within the said Borrough, the slave or slaves so offending shall be Committed to prison for Twelve Hours or be whipped at the discretion of the Mayor, Recorder or any one of the Aldermen before whom such offender shall be brought, And if any White, or other person shall be Guilty of the like offence, such person shall forfeit & pay Five Shillings Proclamation money on Conviction before the Mayor, Recorder or any one of the Aldermen. And in case the offender Neglect or Refuse to pay the said fine, The Major, Recorder or Alderman before whom he is convicted, shall and may Order such offender to be put into the Stocks for any time not exceeding Six Hours. PROVIDED ALWAYS, That it shall and may be lawful for the Mayor, Recorder or Alderman before whom any slave belonging to a Stranger shall be brought, to remit such punishment for the first offence.

Lennon and Kellam, *Wilmington Town Book*, 160, 168-169.

When slaves from the surrounding countryside congregated in the towns on Sunday, enjoying their traditional day off from work, the potential for disturbance escalated accordingly. Local law enforcement authorities were instructed to be particularly vigilant on that day. Special cages were constructed in Wilmington and New Bern for the temporary incarceration of disruptive or recalcitrant bondsmen.

CHAPTER X.

An Act for the better regulating the Town of Wilmington and for confirming and establishing the late Survey of the same, with the Plan annexed. [. . .]

VI. [. . .] the Commissioners of the said Town, for the Time being, are hereby impowered to pass such Orders as they may judge proper [. . .] for preventing all irregular Mobbs and Cabals by Negroes and others, especially on Sundays, for the more effectually bringing to Justice all such Criminals and Offenders against the Laws of this Province, and also for preserving the Peace and Safety of the said Town, and also for preserving the Peace and Safety of the said Town, by appointing proper Guards or Watches in the said Town, [. . .]

Laws of North Carolina, 1745, in Walter Clark, ed., *The State Records of North Carolina*, 16 vols. (11-26) (Raleigh: State of North Carolina, 1895-1906), XXIII:234-235.

On Monday the Twenty nineth day of January in the year of our Lord one thousand Seven hundred and Sixty five. The Mayor, Aldermen and Freeholders of the Borough of Wilmington Convened in Common Council at the Court house therein. [. . .]

And Be it further Ordained by the authority aforesaid, That if after the tenth day of February next following the passing of this Ordinance any number slaves exceeding Three shall be seen together in the Streets, alleys, Vacant Lots, House or other parts within this Borrough, playing, Riotting, or Caballing on the Lords Day commonly called Sunday, or on any other day, or in the night time of any Day, whereby the Inhabitants or any of them may be disturbed or mollested, the slave or slaves so offending shall be immediately apprehended, pursued and taken, by any person or persons discovering the same, and shall by the Mayor, Recorder or any one of the Aldermen be Committed or whiped, or both, as the said Mayor, Recorder or Aldermen shall order and direct.

Lennon and Kellam, *Wilmington Town Book*, 160, 168.

Ordered that John Smith, James Farrow, James Garrett and Jacob Albright be appointed patrolers for the Town of Edenton, and that they be injoined to go to the House of each and every House Holder and Holders of Slaves and Return an Account of the Number of Men and Women Slaves and the young Slaves Setting forth the names of all the Slaves so taken, And also an Account of all the Men and Women Slaves who hire themselves, and Wives and of Slaves who remain or are in town whose Owners Live in the Country that all Negroes Coming under the direction of the Law be hired out for Twenty Days And notice be given the owners and the Patrolers are to apprehend all Negroes who be Long to the Country (Not belonging to the Town) who shall be found in the said Town on Sunday Where any number above three shall be found to Gather and Give Each Twenty Lashes well Layed on the Bare Back unless such Negroes are into Town to Attend Divine Service Or Marketing <*with a Note*> or on his Owners Business with a Note from the Master or Mistress or Overseer and that he or she Depart the Town before Eleven OClock and such as Attend Divine Service depart the Town before three Oclock in the afternoon.

Minutes of the Chowan County Court of Pleas and Quarter Sessions, June 1783, State Archives, Office of Archives and History, Raleigh.

Present Corns. Harnett, Jno. Burgwin, Moses John DeRosset, Wm. Campbell.

Whereas it is necessary that a Cage be built for the Confinement of Negroes committing of any Offences.

And William Campbell Esquire having Agreed to Build the Same. Ordered that the Same be Accordingly built Adjoining on the Eastward of the pilory in Wilmington The Diminsions to be ten feet by ten. And that the Same be paid out of the County Taxes.

Minutes of the New Hanover County Court of Pleas and Quarter Sessions, June 1767, State Archives, Office of Archives and History, Raleigh.

Whereas, In order to prevent the disturbances and riots occasioned by the assembling of Negroes, in the Town particularly on Sundays, (be it ordained that any one Commissioner, or the Town Sergeant be empowered to call such assistance as may be necessary to disperce such meetings, and they are also empower'd, when any Negroes may be particularly noisy or riotous to confine them in the Cage, any time not exceeding twelve hours and if any Negroe should, in consequence of riotous behaviour, be thought to deserve corporal punishment, they shall be taken before some Justice of the peace, or the Intendant, who shall direct such punishment, not exceeding twenty lashes on their bare back by the hand of the Town Sergeant for which service he shall be paid ten shillings by the owner of such slaves.)

New Bern Town Minutes, June 15, 1799, Commissioners' Minutes, Town of New Bern, 1797-1825, State Archives, Office of Archives and History, Raleigh.

Slaves often possessed independent incomes that revealed a surprising latitude of action in a repressive environment. They bought, sold, and bartered firewood, provisions, and various types of merchandise, all contrary to law unless they had permission from their masters to engage in such transactions. Neither provincial legislation nor town ordinances stifled the "pernicious practice" of dealing with blacks, much to the frustration of William Hooper of Wilmington. Occasionally, the Wilmington town commissioners fined whites who engaged in illicit trade with bondsmen.

CHAPTER XXVIII.

An Act for the Better Regulation of the Town of Edenton. [. . .]

And whereas the regulations heretofore made to prevent dealing and trafficking with slaves, have been found insufficient to prevent that dangerous and pernicious practice:

XXIV. Be it Enacted by the authority aforesaid, That if any free person shall either buy from or sell to any slave or slaves within the limits of the said town, or shall barter with any slave or slaves any kind of goods or commodities whatsoever or other thing, without a permission in writing from the master or mistress, or any other person having the management of such slave or slaves, every such person shall on conviction before any justice of the peace of the said county of Chowan, forfeit and pay the sum of ten pounds, to be levied of his or her property as other recoveries by law for the use of the said town, subject nevertheless to the appeal of the party grieved; [. . .]

Laws, 1787, in Clark, *State Records*, XXIV:915, 920.

AS *several Persons in this Town make a practice to purchase from my Negroes whatever they pillage from my House in town or Plantation below, and I have certain information of rum having been sold them and am no stranger to those who are concerned; I give this notice that I will for the future prosecute any person so offending against the Laws of the Province with the utmost rigour.*

WILLIAM HOOPER.

Cape Fear Mercury (Wilmington), September 22, 1773.

Wednesday August 19th 1772. At a Meeting of the Commissioners, Present:

> Archd Maclaine
> John Ancrum
> Richard Player
> Samuel Campbell, Commissioners.

ORDERED, that Mrs. L. Blackmore be fined for dealing with a Negroe fellow contrary to Law, and that the fine she shall pay shall be Forty Shillings, Procl money.

Lennon and Kellam, *Wilmington Town Book*, 211.

PUBLIC NOTICE.

THE inhabitants of the town of Edenton being determined, after the 5th of August next, to take up all negroes bringing or exposing any thing for sale, or purchasing any kind of goods, or trafficking in any manner whatever, without a permission in writing (expressing the articles exposed for sale, and those wanted to purchase) from their master or mistress — hereby give notice that all those who transgress may depend on being prosecuted to the utmost rigour of the law.

Edenton, July 29, 1789.

State Gazette of North Carolina (Edenton), July 30, 1789.

Be it Ordained that from and after the third Instant, no Free person or Slave shall sell or offer for sale in any of the Streets, or on any of the public Wharves or Public Market of this Town, any Bread, Cakes, beer, or Fruit of any kind whatever, or any other Article of any discription, unless they have a licence from the Clerk of the Commissioners, [. . .]

New Bern Town Minutes, September 1, 1800, State Archives.

Bondsmen engaged in sundry trades independent of the direction and control of their masters, generally by hiring themselves either with their masters' consent or in their spare time. Towns tried to restrict the practice. In addressing the issue of slave hire in Wilmington, Washington, Edenton, and Fayetteville, the General Assembly in 1785 claimed that allowing bondsmen from the country or in the towns to work for themselves, and paying their masters a stipulated wage, led to robberies and deprived poor whites of the opportunity of earning a living. Thus the legislature required slaves who worked in the towns to provide written permission from their masters, wear a badge, and pay a tax. Upon learning that country slaves hired their services by the day in town, New Bern town commissioners in 1800 also required badges for bondsmen who hired themselves.

Mary a Slave belonging to Mrs. Deborah Smith being brought into Court, And it being Proved that the said Mary Gives her service of her Mistress and keeps a Tipling House in this for the Entertainment of slaves, contrary to the Act of Assembly.

Ordered that Mr. John C. Bryan do hire out the said Mary at vendue this Evening to Labour for Twenty Days for the Benefit of the Poor.

Minutes of the Craven County Court of Pleas and Quarter Sessions, June 1777, State Archives, Office of Archives and History, Raleigh.

On Monday the Twenty nineth day of January in the year of our Lord one thousand Seven hundred and Sixty five. The Mayor, Alderman and Freeholders of the Borrough of Wilmington Convened in Common Council at the Court house therein. [. . .]

And Be it further ordained by the Authority aforesaid, That no person or persons whatever within this Borrough or the Liberties thereof shall either directly or indirectly suffer or permit his, her or their slave or slaves as aforesaid to take in any work or do any job or jobs of work of any kind whatsoever or suffer or permit any such slave or slaves to follow any Trade, mistery or Occupation, except under the direction of the said owner or possessor of such slave or of some other white person, to the Intent that no slave or slaves whatever shall have or receive any benefit to him her or themselves, but to the particular use and benefit of the Master or owner of such slave under the penalty of Thirty five Shillings proclamation money for each and every offence to be recovered and applied as other fines are by this Ordinance directed.

Lennon and Kellam, *Wilmington Town Book*, 160, 167.

CHAPTER VI.

An Additional Act to Amend the Several Acts for Regulating the Town of Wilmington, and to Regulate and Restrain the Conduct of Slaves and Others in the Said Town, and in the Towns of Washington, Edenton and Fayetteville. [. . .]

V. [. . .] And whereas it is customary for many persons, as well in the country as in the several towns in this State, to permit their slaves to hire themselves out from day to day, by which great profits are acquired, and it is reasonable that those persons who derive such advantages from the labour of their slaves in the towns should contribute more than the ordinary taxes towards its support, and at the same time that a distinction should be made between such slaves as may be returned as taxable property in the said towns respectively, and such whose owners reside in the country, and return their taxable property there, although part of their slaves generally work in the towns. And whereas permitting slaves to hire themselves under proper restrictions and regulations, may be rendered convenient for such persons as may occasionally want daily labourers:

VI. Be it therefore Enacted by the authority aforesaid, That from and after the first day of May next, it shall not be lawful for any slave in the towns of Wilmington, Washington, Edenton or Fayetteville, to hire her or himself out, without first producing a permission in writing from the owner, or other persons having the care or management of such slave, directed to the commissioners, trustees or directors of the town where such slave shall be; who thereupon shall cause the said permission to be entered by the town clerk in their books and filed, for which the owner of the slave shall pay a fee of one shilling; and the commissioners shall cause a leaden or pewter badge to be affixed to some conspicuous part of the outer garment of such slave with a device, which may be altered from time to time, expressive of the intention of such badge; and every slave having a badge in manner by this Act directed, may hire him or herself out, and may lawfully be hired by any person or persons whatever.

VII. And be it Enacted by the authority aforesaid, That for all slaves who shall have badges as above directed, and who shall be town taxables, there shall be paid as follows, to wit, For every male slave being a tradesman there shall be paid yearly to the commissioners, trustees or directors the sum of sixteen shillings; for every male slave not being a tradesman the sum of ten shillings, and for every female slave the sum of eight shillings; but if any slaves having such badges shall not be returned as town taxables, then there shall be paid for every male slave being a tradesman twenty-four shillings; for every male slave not being a tradesman the sum of fifteen shillings, and for every female slave twelve shillings, to be applied as other taxes assessed and collected in the said towns.

Laws, 1785, in Clark, *State Records*, XXIV:725, 726-727.

Whereas many Negroes come out of the country and work by the day, to the injury and inconvenience of persons owning Negroes in Town. It is therefore Orderd that all Negroes who hire out by the day, shall have a bage, sewed or otherwise fastened to their outside garment which Badge the Clerk is hereby directed to grant to the person applying on their producing an Order from the Treasurer for that purpose, for which the person applying must pay five shillings. <*If any Negro Slave shall offend*> If any Slave shall fail to Comply with the foregoing Order, they shall for each offence be liable to be whipped not exceedied ten lashes, and be sold to the highest bidder by the Town Sergeant for the term of one weeke, the money ariseing therefrom to be applied for the use of the Town.

New Bern Town Minutes, September 19, 1800, State Archives.

———————

Some slaves also lived independently, occupying houses or outbuildings in the towns, including Wilmington and Edenton. While some slaves utilized the lodgings of their masters, who might have been away on business or who resided in country homes, other bondsmen possessed the means to rent dwellings. Legislation by the General Assembly, ordinances by town commissioners, and directives by county courts prohibited slaves from renting quarters in the towns and imposed fines on whites who permitted the practice. Few substantive changes followed. Such punitive practices undoubtedly proved no more successful than efforts to curb boisterous behavior among some slaves or interdict illicit trade between blacks and whites.

CHAPTER XLIX.

An Act to Amend an Act, Intituled, "An Act for the Regulation of the Town of Wilmington." [. . .]

IX. [. . .] That the commissioners of the said town are hereby particularly required and directed to make the necessary regulations to prevent slaves from keeping houses in the said town, and to impose fines and penalties on the owners and tenants of houses who shall suffer the same to be occupied by slaves, [. . .]

Laws, 1784, in Clark, *State Records*, XXIV:618, 621.

On Monday the Twenty nineth day of January in the year of our Lord one thousand Seven hundred and Sixty five. The Mayor, Alderman and Freeholders of the Borrough of Wilmington Convened in Common Council at the Court house therein. [. . .]

AND WHEREAS many persons possessed of Negroes and other slaves for a certain stipulated Gratuity or sum of money, to be paid them weekly or otherwise by such slaves, do permit their said slaves to hire houses, Tenements, Kitchens and Outhouses and to live at large; which tends greatly to promote Idleness, Revelling and disturbance, Thieving and Stealing and many other crimes within this Borrough. For remedy whereof for the future — Be It Ordained by the authority aforesaid, That, no person whatsoever being an Owner or actually possessed by hire or otherwise of any slaves or slaves shall for any gratuity or consideration whatever suffer or permit any such slave or slaves either directly or indirectly to hire any House, Outhouse or Tenement or any part or parcele of any House, Outhouse or Tenement within the Borough of Wilmington, [. . .]

Lennon and Kellam, *Wilmington Town Book*, 160, 166.

Ordered that no Slave or Slaves shall be allowed to keep in that Town [Edenton] any Houses, and that such Person or Persons to whom such Slave or Slaves, who keep such Houses do belong take the said Slaves to their own Habitations; it having been found by long experience that the suffering Slaves to keep Houses of their Own is a very great nusiance;—It is likewise Ordered that the Constables and Patrollers of the Town of Edenton, do see this Order well and faithfully put into Execution.

Minutes of the Chowan County Court of Pleas and Quarter Sessions, March 1775, State Archives.

Free African Americans

North Carolina's free African American population consisted of manumitted slaves, runaways passing as free, and immigrant free blacks from other colonies, principally Virginia. North Carolina, in 1715, tried to discourage the presence of free blacks by requiring liberated slaves to leave the province within six months of their manumission. The General Assembly permitted freed bondsmen to remain in the colony, provided the county courts approved their manumission, in 1741. Among the slaves manumitted were those who purchased their freedom. Amelia Green, perhaps allowed to hire her services or sell garden produce, saved money not only to buy her own freedom but that of her child. Adding to the free black population were runaway slaves like Pompy, who claimed to be free, and immigrants. Late in the eighteenth century the legislature, concerned about slave revolts abroad and the increasing number of free black immigrants in the state, required free blacks and manumitted slaves to post bond for their proper conduct or risk being sold as slaves.

State of North Carolina New Hanover County.

Know all Men by these presents, That I Isabella Chapman, of the County of New Hanover in the State of North Carolina for and in Consideration of the Sum of One Hundred pounds Current Money of the State of North Carolina to me in hand paid by a Certain Negroe woman Named Amelia formerly the property of Robert Schaw, Esqr. of Brunswick County Deceassd But Now Become free by her Purchasing of her freedom from the said Robert Schaw. Since which purchase her Freedom has Been confirmed and Established to hereby by Act of the General Assembly of the State of North Carolina, and by which said Law or Act she is now known and calld by the Name of Amelia Green; thereupon for Said Consideration Money I do hereby Acknowledge and to be fully contented and paid for A Certain Negroe or mollato Girl Named Princess the Daughter of her the Said Amelia Green by me this day Sold to the Said Negroe woman Amelia Green as aforesaid Which Said mollato Girl Princess Devolved to me by the Last will and Testatment Of Owner Shaw, late of Brunswick County, Deceased. Have Hereby Bargaind and sold and by those presents do Bargain and sell Unto her the Said Amelia Green the Said Mallato Girl her Daughter Princess above Mentioned to have and to hold the Said Mollato Girl Princess by these presents Bargained and sold unto her the Said Amelia Green and to her Hiers and assignes for Ever, And I the Said Isabella Chapman for myself my Heirs Executors administrators and assignes the Said Mollato Girl Princess by these presents Bargained and sold unto the Said Negroe woman Amelia Green as aforesaid Against me the Said Isabella Chapman my heirs etc. and against all and Every other person and Persons whatever Shall and will Warrant and forever Defend by these presents in Witness Whereof I have hereunto Sett my hand and seal this Twenty first Day of March In the Year of Our Lord One thousand Seven Hundred and Ninety Six 1796.

I Chapman

the word Green in the fifth Line
from the Bottom was first unterlined
Before signed.
Witness Alexr. Schaw.

[*Endorsed*:]
Isabella Chapman to Amelia Green Registered in the Records
of New Hanover County Book I page 223. March the 25th 1796
R. Bradley Register

Received the Consideration money within mentioned in full this Twenty first day of March in the year one thousand Seven Hundred and Ninety Six. 1796.
Witness. Alexr. Schaw

I Chapman

New Hanover County March [*illegible*] 1796
The Execution of the within Bill Sale was proved by the Oath
of Alexr. Schaw and ordered to be registered
Geo: Gibbs [*illegible*]

Isabella Chapman to Amelia Green, March 21, 1796, Slave Collection, State Archives, Office of Archives and History, Raleigh.

March 23, 1799

TWENTY DOLLARS REWARD.

RAN-AWAY the 23d day of February last, a Mulatto Man a slave, named POMPY, the property of the subscriber; had on when he went away, a brown broad cloth coat, a stolen light coloured great coat; he also stole a Mare, Bridle and Saddle, which mare he has since exchanged for a sorrel mare, on the north side of Cape-Fear river. He passes by the name of JAMES BUTLER, a freeman; [. . .]

THOMAS STANBACK.

Richmond County, March 19.

Advertisement in *The North Carolina Minerva and Fayetteville Advertiser*, in Freddie L. Parker, ed., *Stealing a Little Freedom: Advertisements for Slave Runaways in North Carolina, 1791-1840* (New York: Garland Publishing Co., 1994), 95.

CHAP. XVI.

An Act *to prevent any person who may emigrate from any of the West-India or Bahama Islands, or the French, Dutch or Spanish settlements on the southern coast of America, from bringing slaves into this state, and also for imposing certain restrictions on free persons of colour who may hereafter come into this state.* [. . .]

III. *And be it further enacted,* That if any free person of colour shall come into this state, by land or water, or any slave shall hereafter be emancipated, he, she or they shall be compelled to give bond and security to the Sheriff, payable to the Governor for the use of the state, in the sum of two hundred pounds, for his, her of their good behaviour, during the time he, she or they may remain in this state; [. . .]

Laws of the State of North-Carolina, 1795, c. 16.

———

Among the slaves to be manumitted were those owned by free blacks, who often sought to liberate their bondsmen. The number of free black slave owners was always small, but many, including Jemima Barrs and Thomas Sylvester, deliberately purchased spouses and children with the intention of freeing them. One of the most prosperous freedmen in the state, John Caruthers Stanly, opened a barber shop in New Bern;

bought several plantations; and owned numerous slaves and manumitted several, including his wife. Stanly, whose liberation the General Assembly confirmed in 1798, was the son of an African-born Ibo woman and New Bern merchant John Wright Stanly.

CHAP. LXXVI.

An Act *to emancipate Jack, alias Jack Small, a person of colour.*

WHEREAS, Jemima Barrs, a free-woman of mixed blood, hath represented to this General Assembly, that she hath purchased a certain Jack Small, for a valuable consideration, and since hath become his legal wife: And whereas the said Jemima Barrs hath petitioned this General Assembly to emancipate and set free her said husband, Jack Small aforesaid:

I. *Be it therefore enacted by the General Assembly of the state of North-Carolina, and it is hereby enacted by the authority of the same,* That the aforesaid person of colour Jack Small, shall henceforth be emancipated and absolutely set free, by the name of Jack Small; and be entitled to all the privileges and immunities which free people of colour enjoy and possess in this state, any law to the contrary notwithstanding. *Provided nevertheless.* That nothing in this act contained shall affect the claim or claims of any other person or persons, either in law or equity, except the claim of the said Jemima Barrs.

Laws, 1794, c. 76.

To the Worshipful the County Court of Pleas and Quarter Sessions for Pasquotank County The Petition of Thomas Sylvester a Freeman of colour whom Humbly Sheweth.

That he some years agoe took to Wife a Negroe Woman Slave by the name of Joan the property of a certain Jeremiah Symons who hath borne him four Children, to wit, Abba, Nancey, Jerry and Annaritta that by the Assistance, Industry economy and prudence of his said Wife Joan he hath been enabled to raise a sufficient Sum to purchase her and her Children from their said Master.

May it therefore please your Worships taking your Petitioners Case under your consideration to pass an Order for the liberation and emancipation of the said Joan, Abba, Nancey, Jerry and Annaritta by the Names of Joan Sylvester, Abba Sylvester, Nancey Sylvester, Jerry Sylvester and Annaritta Sylvester agreeable to the Power and Authority in your Worship vested by the Act of the General Assembly in such Cases made and provided And Your Petitioner as in duty bound shall ever pray.

Will Blair for the Petitioner

Petition of Thomas Sylvester, Minutes of the Pasquotank County Court of Pleas and Quarter Sessions, June 1797, State Archives, Office of Archives and History, Raleigh; Pasquotank County, Miscellaneous Records, Records of Slaves and Free Persons of Color, Bonds and Petitions to Free Slaves, State Archives, Office of Archives and History, Raleigh.

To all persons to whom these presents shall come Greeting

Know the that Alexander Stewart and Lydia Stewart his wife both of Newbern Craven County and State of North Carolina for and in consideration of the faithful and meritorious services of a certain mulatto boy slave hitherto to them belonging named John alias John Stanly and by authority and in pursuance of a licence for this purpose to them granted by the county court of Craven have given granted and confirmed and by these presents do give grant and confirm unto the said Mulatto boy John alias John Stanly his freedom liberty and emancipation. [. . .]

Alexr. Stewart
Lydia Stewart

Deed of emancipation of John Stanly, April 20, 1795, Slave Collection, State Archives.

CHAP. CXII.

An Act *to emancipate certain persons therein named.*

WHEREAS Alexander Stewart and Lydia his wife, have by deed under their hands and seals; given, granted and confirmed unto John Caruthers Stanly, a person of mixed blood, heretofore their slave, his freedom, as a reward for his meritorious services; And whereas the said John Caruthers Stanly is desirous of having his emancipation confirmed by law. And whereas Amelia Green, a free woman of colour, has petitioned this General Assembly, to emancipate her daughter Princess Green;

I. *Be it therefore enacted by the General Assembly of the state of North-Carolina, and it is hereby enacted by the authority of the same.* That the said John Caruthers Stanly and Princess Green by the said names, are hereby emancipated and set free; and the said persons hereby liberated, and each of them are hereby declared to be able and capable in law; to possess and enjoy every right, privilege and immunity, in as full and ample manner as they could or might have done if they had been born free.

Laws, 1798, c. 112.

However, early North Carolina records suggest that the offspring of interracial unions between unmarried white women (often indentured servants and apprentices) and black men, and the children of free African American women accounted for the preponderance of free blacks in the colony. Such single women occasionally bore several children. The Bertie County court in 1763 apprenticed four children of free mulatto Betty James. Illegitimate mulatto children were apprenticed to age thirty-one, later reduced to twenty-one, as opposed to twenty-one and eighteen for white boys and girls respectively.

Orderd that Pattey the Daughter of Betty James a Free Mulatoe about Eight years of age be bound to Richard Bell and Mary his Wife til she Arrive at the age of Twenty one Years.

Ordered that Nanny the Daughter of Betty James a Free Mulattoe about the age of Ten Years be Bound to Ephraim Weston til she Arrive at the age of Twenty one Years.

Orderd that Davy the Soon of Betty James a Free Mulatoe about the age of four Years be Bound to Ephraim Weston to learn the Trade of a Cordwainer until he Arrive at the Age of Twenty one Years.

Ordered that Tom the soon of Bett James a Free Mulatoe about the age of Six Years be Bound to John Moore to larn the Trade of a Cordwainer untill he arrive at the Age of Twenty one Years.

Minutes of the Bertie County Court of Pleas and Quarter Sessions, May 1763, State Archives, Office of Archives and History, Raleigh.

At the instance of William Dawson Esqr. and the mother of Anthony Berry a mullatoe Child the said mullatoe is hereby Bound to the Said William Dawson under the Law untill the said Child arrives to the age of thirty one Years the mother of the Said Child haveing Confessed in open Court that she was a Servant when the said Mullotoe Child was Begot and Born.

Minutes of the Cumberland County Court of Pleas and Quarter Sessions, January 1758, State Archives, Office of Archives and History, Raleigh.

On Motion of Mr. Caswell Ordered that John Heylyn Aged Nine Years and Mary Heylyn aged Seven Years (being Base Born Molatto Children) be Bound to Samuel Smith untill they Arrive to the Age of Twenty One Years, the Boy to be learned the Calling of a Cooper and the Girl House Work and Seamstress.

Minutes of the Craven County Court of Pleas and Quarter Sessions, June 1770, State Archives, Office of Archives and History, Raleigh.

Free black or mulatto apprentices, as well as whites, sometimes suffered at the hands of their masters. Thomas Carter appealed to the Cumberland County court to protect his grandchildren. Aggrieved apprentices like Jenny Spellman sometimes ran away from their masters. If, like William Allin, they were apprehended, they served additional time at the end of their indentures to compensate their masters for the loss of their labor and the cost of their capture. Nicholas Edwin obtained a certificate from the Rowan County court to document the fulfillment of the terms of his apprenticeship and to warrant that he was a free man.

At the Instance of Thomas Carter a mullatoe Grand father to Abraham Carter an Infant mullatoe the Grandson of the said Thomas and Now in the Keeping of James Wright the Said abraham is by order of Court Bound to Plunkett Ballard of said County attorney at Law and the Clerk of this Court is ordered [*illegible*] and Indentures to the Said Ballard accordingly [*torn*] ordered that the High Sheriff of the Said County take the said a[braham] Carter out of the possession of the Said

Wright and to Deliver [*torn*] Ballard. And upon the further Complaint of the said [*torn*] that the said James Wright unlawfully Detains and Ill[*torn*] Luick anney and moses Carter Samuell Carter and Elizabeth C[arter] [*torn*] More of his Grand Children Mullatoes It is therefore ordere[d] [*torn*] High Sheriff of the Said County take the Possession of the Sa[id] [*torn*] four Mullatoe Children and Safely keep them so as to produce [*torn*] Next Succeeding Court to be held for the Said County.

Minutes of the Cumberland County Court of Pleas and Quarter Sessions, January 1758, State Archives.

Advertisements.

Newbern, July 19th, 1764.

RAN away from the Subscriber, a Free Negroe Wench, named Jenny Spellman. Whoever secures her, shall receive Twenty Shillings Reward. And as she is bound to me by Indenture for a Term of Years, yet unexpired, whoever harbours or entertains her, will be prosecuted with Rigour.

RICHARD FENNER.

North Carolina Magazine; or, Universal Intelligencer (New Bern), July 20, 1764.

On Motion of John Demm Esqr.

Ordered the Court that William Allin a Molatto Boy Serve James Hemphill 4 Months and a half Exclusive of his Said Indenture for the Time that he was Absent from his Said Masters Serve. etc.

Minutes of the Rowan County Court of Pleas and Quarter Sessions, October 1768, State Archives, Office of Archives and History, Raleigh.

This is to Certify to all persons whom it may Concern, that Whereas the Bearer hereof a Negroe man named Nicholas Edwin was bound an apprentice to the late Thomas parker Esqr. deceased and as such has behaved himself during his Service to the said Thomas parker Esqr. and his heirs, and now know the, that Thomas Frohock, having the said Negroe man named Nicholas Edwin in my possession do find him the said Nicholas to be at this Time a Freeperson and do hereby discharge him of his said Service and Recommend him to all persons as such according as his Merit shall deserve Given under my hand and Seal this 5th day of August 1774.

Minutes of the Rowan County Court of Pleas and Quarter Sessions, August 1774, State Archives.

Free blacks suffered civil discriminations beyond those of lengthier apprenticeships. Particularly onerous for those who remained in North Carolina was discriminatory taxation. Legislation in 1723 subjected white wives of free blacks to the poll tax, the principal means of raising money in North Carolina. No other white women in the colony were taxed. In addition, all free black children, like slaves, were taxed at age twelve, whereas free white girls remained altogether untaxed and free white boys became taxable at age sixteen. White and free black petitioners to the General Assembly pointed out the inequity of such taxation; noted that free blacks and mulattos fulfilled their public responsibilities, such as militia duty and road work; and sought the repeal of objectionable legislation. Although Virginia in 1769 banned the tax on the wives of free blacks, North Carolina demurred.

CHAPTER V.

An Act for an additional Tax on all free Negroes, Mulattoes, Mustees, and such Persons, Male and Female, as now are, or hereafter shall be, intermarried with any such Persons, resident in this Government. [. . .]

II. [. . .] That all free Negroes, Mulattoes, and other Persons of that kind, being mixed Blood, including the Third Generation, who are, or hereafter shall be, Inhabitants or Residents in this Government, both Male and Female, who are of the age of Twelve years and upwards, shall, from the Ratification of this Act, be deemed and taken for Tithables, and as such each and every of them shall, Yearly, pay the same Levies and Taxes as the other Tithable Inhabitants do, [. . .]

Laws of North Carolina, 1723, in Walter Clark, ed., *The State Records of North Carolina*, 16 vols. (11-26) (Raleigh: State of North Carolina, 1895-1906), XXIII:106.

To the Worshipful the Speaker and Gentlemen of the Assembly.
The petition of Sundry of the Inhabitants of the Counties of Northampton Edgecombe and Granville.

HUMBLY SHEWETH

That by one Act of Assembly passed in the year 1723, Intituled "An Act for an Additional Tax on all free Negroes, Mulattoes, Mustees and such Persons Male & Female, as now are or hereafter shall be intermarried with any such Persons resident in this Government." Amongst other Things it was enacted That all free Negroes &c. that were or shou'd thereafter be Inhabitants of this Province Male & Female being of the Age of twelve Years & upwards shou'd be deemed Tythables and as such should yearly pay the same Levies and Taxes as other Tythable Inhabitants.

That many Inhabitants of the sd Counties who are Free Negroes & Mulattoes and persons of Probity & good Demeanor and chearfully contribute towards the Discharge of very public Duty injoined them by Law. But by reason of being obliged by the sd Act of Assembly to pay Levies for their Wives and Daughters as therein mentioned are greatly Impoverished and many of them rendered unable to support themselves and Families with the common Necessaries of Life.

Wherefore your Petitioners would humbly pray in behalf of the sd Free Negroes &c. That so much of the said recited Act as compels such of them as Intermarry with those of their own complection to pay Taxes for their Wives & Daughters may be repealed or that they may be otherwise relieved as to your Worships in your great Wisdom seem meet.

And your Petitioners as in Duty bound shall pray &c. [. . .]

Petition, c. 1763, in William L. Saunders, ed., *The Colonial Records of North Carolina*, 10 vols. (Raleigh: State of North Carolina, 1886-1890), VI:982.

CHAP. XXXVII.

An Act for exempting free negro, mulatto, and Indian women, from the payment of levies. [. . .]

I. [. . .] *Be it enacted, by the Governor, Council, and Burgesses, of this present General Assembly, and it is hereby enacted, by the authority of the same,* That from and after the ninth day of June next, all free negro, mulatto, and

Indian women, and all wives, other than slaves, of free negroes, mulattoes, and Indians, shall be, and are hereby exempted from being listed as tithables, and from the payment of any public, county, or parish levies.

Laws, 1769, in William Waller Hening, ed., *The Statutes at Large; Being a Collection of All the Laws of Virginia*, 13 vols., 2d ed.(Philadelphia: the editor, by Thomas Desilver, 1820-1823), VIII:393.

To the Honorable the Speaker and Gentlemen, of the house of Assembly.

The Petition of the Inhabitants of Granville County Humbly Sheweth that by the Act of Assembly Concerning Tythables it is among other things enacted that all free Negroes and Mulato Women and all wives of free Negroes and Mulatoes are Declard Tythables and Chargable for Defraying the Public County and Parish Leveys of this province which Your Petitioners Humbly Conceive is highly Derogatory of the Rights of Freeborn Subjects.

Your Petitioners therefore Pray that An Act may pass Exempting Such free Negroe and Mulatoe Women and all wives other then Slaves of free Negroes and Mulatoes from being Listed as Tythables and from Paying any Public County or Parish Leveys and Your Petitioners Shall ever pray etc. [. . .]

Petition from the Inhabitants of Granville County to the Speaker and Assembly, November 27, 1771, Petitions rejected or not acted on, Lower House Papers, Session of November-December 1771, General Assembly Session Records, Colonial (Upper and Lower House), State Archives, Office of Archives and History, Raleigh.

Despite such penalties, the law treated free blacks and whites equally in other respects. Free black men voted in North Carolina, at least until a statute in 1715 disenfranchised them. However, the crown disallowed that law, and subsequent legislation and the state constitution of 1776 made no distinction between whites and blacks in terms of suffrage. Free blacks in the state voted until denied the franchise by constitutional amendment in 1835. Unlike Virginia, North Carolina did not relegate free blacks to an inferior status in the militia. Also, free

blacks in North Carolina, like whites, were entitled to exemptions from such public duties as roadwork.

I. We therefore, in the first place, humbly represent to your Lordships, and we do Assert and Maintain, That it is one of the fundamental Rights and unquestionable Priviledges belonging to Englishmen, That all Elections of their Representatives to serve in Parliament, ought to be free and indifferent, without any Prayer of Commandment to the contrary, and that no Alien born out of the Allegiance to the Crown of England, unless he be otherwise especially qualify'd, ought to Elect for, or be Elected to serve as a Member of Assembly; all which, notwithstanding, at the Election of Members of Assembly to serve for Berkly County made in the Month of November, 1701. [. . .] For so it was, may it please your Lordships, that at the said Election, much Threatenings, many Intreaties, and other unjustifiable Actions were made use of, and illegal and unqualify'd votes given in to the Sheriff; and by him Receiv'd and Return'd, particularly the votes of very many unqualify'd Aliens were taken and enter'd, the votes of several Members of the Council were filed and Received, a great number of Servants, and Poor and indigent Persons, voted promiscuously with their Masters and Creditors, as also several free Negroes were Receiv'd, and taken for as good Electors as the best Freeholders in the Province. So that we leave it with your Lordships to Judge, whether admitting Aliens, Strangers, Servants, Negroes, &c. as good and qualify'd voters, can be thought any ways agreeable to King Charle's Patent to your Lordship's, or the English Constitution or Government.

Petition to Lords Proprietors, 1705, in Saunders, *Colonial Records*, II:903.

The Constitution, 1776. [. . .]

Section VII. That all Freeman of the Age of twenty-one Years, who have been Inhabitants of any one County within the State twelve Months immediately preceding the Day of any Election, and possessed of a Freehold within the same County of fifty Acres of Land for six

Months next before and at the Day of Election, shall be entitled to vote for a Member of the Senate.

Section VIII. That all Freeman of the Age of twenty-one Years, who have been Inhabitants of any County within this State twelve Months immediately preceding the day of any Election, and shall have paid public Taxes, shall be entitled to vote for Members of the House of Commons for the County in which he resides.

State Constitution, 1776, in Clark, *State Records*, XXIII:980-981.

CHAP. II.

An Act, for the better Regulation of the Militia. [. . .]

And be it further enacted, That all such free mulattos, negros, or Indians, as are or shall be listed, as aforesaid, shall appear without arms; and may be emploied as drummers, trumpeters, or pioneers, or in such other servile labour, as they shall be directed to perform.

Laws, 1738, in Hening, ed., *The Statutes at Large; . . . Virginia*, V:16-17.

GRANVILLE COUNTY.

MUSTER ROLL OF THE REGIMENT IN GRANVILLE COUNTY, UNDER THE COMMAND OF COLO. WILLIAM EATON, AS TAKEN AT A GENERAL MUSTER OF THE SAID REGIMENT

8 October, 1754 [. . .]

CAPTAIN JOHN GLOVER'S COMPANY, [. . .]

20. Wm. Chavers, Negro.
21. Wm. Chavers, Jun., Mul.
22. Gilbert Chavers, Mulatto. [. . .]
28. Edward Harris, Negro. [. . .]

CAPTAIN OSBORN JEFFREY'S COMPANY [. . .]

The next 5 are Mulattoes:
78. Thomas Gowen.
79. Michael Gowen.
80. Edward Gowen.

81. Robert Davis.
82. William Burnel. [. . .]

Clark, *State Records*, XXII:370-372.

Ordered that Robert Mitchell Free Negroe be Exempt from Working on the Roads being upwards of Sixty Years of Age.

Minutes of the Craven County Court of Pleas and Quarter Sessions, June 1775, State Archives.

To the extent allowed within the existing legal framework, free blacks in early North Carolina led lives that resembled those of average non-slaveholding whites. Some, including Black Dick in Onslow County, died impoverished. But Alexander Fuller's account with the mercantile firm of Nash and McNair in the same county, showing the purchase on credit of shot, powder, thread, cloth, shoes, sugar, and coffee, typified mercantile tabs found throughout the colony. Fuller, a carpenter, enjoyed the confidence of Nash and McNair, and when possible, reduced his outstanding balance by labor and by payments in cash or in kind. Before John Provey joined the British army during the Revolution, he lived in a small, modestly furnished house, owned livestock, and worked a field of Indian corn.

On Motion of John Starkey that Black Dick a free negro Man, is Dead and Owes him £7.3.7 proclamation.

Orderd that Mr. Starkey Sell what he can find Belonging to said Dicks small Effects and pay as far as it will goe to him self and others.

Minutes of the Onslow County Court of Pleas and Quarter Sessions, July 1753, State Archives, Office of Archives and History, Raleigh.

Alexander Fuller (a Mulatto Carpenter) To Nash and McNair

		[£. s. d.]	[£. s. d.]
1763			6
Sept. 9	To 1/2 Bushel Salt		
Octr. 13	To 1 1/2 yards Cotton 4/4		6. 6
Novr. 14	1 lb. Powder	5. 4	
	4 lb. Shott	2. 8	8.
Decr. 27	1 lb. Coffee	2.	
	2 lb. Sugar	2.	
	1 pr. woms Shoes	10.	
	1 pr. Scissors	1. 4	15. 4
31	3 1/2 yards Bearskin 12/	2. 2.	
	1/2 yard Shalloon	1. 8	
	2 doz. Bullets 1/8	3. 4	
	1 oz. whited Brd thread	1.	
	2 Sticks [Mo]hair	1. 4	
	1 oz. Colerd thread	8	
1764	6 yards Check 3/6	1. 1.	3. 11.
	2 1/2 yards Duroy 3/6	8. 9	
Jany. 2	1/2 yard Muslin 6/4	3. 2	
	4 1/2 yards Dowlass 2/4	10. 6	
	1/2 bushel Salt	8.	
	8 yards Tape	1.	1. 8.
[. . .]			
1765	Do. Fuller Cr.		
Decr. 31	By work done on a Stable, which was to have been £4 — but as he did not complete it allow him		3.
	Ballce due to N & M procl. £		19 . 1 . 7

Account of Alexander Fuller with Nash and McNair, 1763-1764, Onslow County, Miscellaneous Records, Slave (Civil Actions Concerning), State Archives, Office of Archives and History, Raleigh.

Estimate of Losses sustained by John Provey on Account of his Attachment to the British Government.

To 2 Horses, which he left behind him when he left his Home, with the View of joining the King's Army — £10.0.0

To a small Field of Indian Corn, Potatoes etc. . . . .

To a Dozen grown Fowls . . . .

To a Dozen young Ducks . . . .

To a small dwelling House . . . .

To a Bed, and Household Furniture . . . .

To a House, built upon Rebel Ground at New York, by Permission of the Mayor [David Matthews] (with a large Garden well fenced in) the Materials of which, with the wages of Artificers and Labourers, at the lowest Computation, exceeded two Hundred Pounds New york Currency.

Loyalist Claim of John Provey, in Audit Office 13/123. British Records, State Archives, Office of Archives and History, Raleigh.

John Provey exemplified a number of free blacks, who, along with slaves, joined the British in the American Revolution. During the war, Provey served in the Company of Black Pioneers and went to New York, where he built a house and expected to remain. The British defeat ultimately found him in England, where he became one of forty-seven blacks who sought restitution from the Loyalist Claims Commission for property lost as a result of their allegiance to Great Britain. Like half of the blacks, he obtained nothing; the others received a pittance. By contrast, most whites received some assistance, and almost always more than the most fortunate African American. The claims commissioners doubted that the blacks had been free before the war and, in any case, felt that they should be fortunate to have their liberty. Thus petitions by blacks seldom received serious consideration.

Decision.

This Application is perfectly unfounded because instead of suffering by the War (for he hardly states any Losses of Property) he is a gainer by it For he is in a much better Country where he may with

Industry get his Bread and where he can never more be a Slave for notwithstanding he pretends to have been born free We cannot easily give Credit to that it being the common tale of them all.

Such applications hardly deserve a serious Investigation or a serious Answer However we think it our Duty in all Cases (however trifling) which come before us to state to the Lords of the Treasury those Reasons which induce us to think that the Parties are not proper Objects of the Bounty of Government.

In such a Case as this We trust it will not be necessary to say more than that there is not the smallest Color to consider this Man as an American Sufferer and of Course that he ought not to receive any allowance.

Loyalist Claim of John Provey, in Audit Office 12/101. British Records, State Archives, Office of Archives and History, Raleigh.

While Provey's freedom, at least, seemed secure, free blacks in North Carolina, struggling to survive amid an overwhelmingly white society, faced an ongoing threat of bodily theft and sale as slaves. Legislation in 1741 required the liberation of free inhabitants who had been enslaved beyond the colonies and brought to America. Hence, Peter Charles secured his liberty at the order of the Craven County court. But in North Carolina, free blacks—the children of Ann Driggus, and Dolley James herself, for example—might be seized and sold into bondage. Certificates of freedom offered no guarantee against enslavement. Tardily, North Carolina legislation in 1778 forbade the enslavement of free blacks. Yet as the number of free blacks increased in the state, so did the chance of losing that precious freedom.

CHAPTER XXIV.

An Act Concerning Servants and Slaves. [. . .]

XXIII. And be it further Enacted, by the Authority aforesaid, That if any Person or Persons already have, or shall hereafter, import into this Government, and here sell or retain; for his own Use as a Slave, any Person or Persons that shall have been free in any Christian Country,

Island or Plantation, or Turk or Moor, in Amity with his Majesty, such Importer or Seller as aforesaid shall forfeit and pay to the Party, from whom the said free Person shall recover his or her Freedom double the Sum for which such free Person was sold; [. . .]

Laws, 1741, in Clark, *State Records*, XXIII:191, 196.

Peter Charles having heretofore complained against John Edge Tomlinson alledging that the said Charles is an East India Indian and Free Born, and being detained as a Slave by the said John Edge Tomlinson, [. . .]

Ordered that the same be continued for Trial at the next Court, [. . .] Peter Charles vs. John Edge Tomlinson. Petition for Freedom etc.

This Cause being Ruled for Trial this Day, the Court proceeded to Hear the Parties and upon the Examination of Witnesses. The Court was Unanimously of Opinion that the said Peter Charles is an East India Indian, and justly Intitled to his Freedom, Therefore Ordered that he be Immediately Discharged and Set Free, and that the Defendant John Edge Tomlinson pay all Costs.

Minutes of the Craven County Court of Pleas and Quarter Sessions, September 1777, State Archives.

BROAD CREEK, *on Neuse River, April* 9.

ON Saturday night, *April* the 4th, broke into the house of the subscriber at the head of *Green's Creek*, where I had some small property under the care of *Ann Driggus*, a free negro woman, two men in disguise, who with masks on their faces, and clubs in their hands, beat and wounded her terribly and carried away four of her children, three girls and a boy, the bigest of said girls got off in the dark and made her escape, one of the girl's name is *Becca*, and the other *Charita*, the boy is named *Shadrack*; she says the men were *William Munday* and *Charles Towzer*, a sailor lately from *Newbern*, these men were on board of a boat belonging to *Kelly Cason*, and was with him in the boat about the middle of the day. Fifty dollars reward will be given to any person who will stop the children and apprehend the robbers so that they may be brought to justice.

JOHN CARUTHERS.

North Carolina Gazette (New Bern), April 10, 1778.

Know all men by these presents that we Lemuel Sawyer John Carter Richard Mullin of Perquimans County in North Carolina are held and firmly Bound unto Thomas Hosea Sheriff in the Just and full Sum of one Thousand pounds Currency for the which payment will and Truly to be made we bind our Selves our Heirs Executors and Administrators Jointly and Severly firmly by these presents Sealed with our Seals and Dated this 19th Day of February 1799.

The Condition of the above obligation is Such that if the above Bound in Lemuel Sawyer Shall personally be and appear Before the Justices of the County Court of pleas and Quarter Sessions held for the County of Perquimans at the Court House in the Town and Hertford on the Second Monday in May Next then and there To answer unto Dolley James a free Girl of Coulor under the age of Twenty one years by Asher Clayton her next friend in a plea wherefore with force and arms he Assaulted beat and for a Long time To wit the Space of Seven Days un lawfully faulsly and without Cause Imprisoned her with Intent To Convey her into foreign parts and Sell and Dispose of her as a Slave etc. etc. etc. and other wrongs to her did to her Damage Five Hundred pounds then and there to Stand to and abide by the Judgment of the Said Court thereon and not to Depart without Liberty first had and obtained then the above obligation to be void otherwise to be and Remain in full force and virtue Signd. Sealed and Delivered In the presents of

Lemuel Sawyer (Seal)
John Carter (Seal)
Richard Mullin (Seal)

T. Baleman

Perquimans County, Miscellaneous Records, Slave Records, Civil and Criminal Cases, State Archives, Office of Archives and History, Raleigh.

North Carolina Perqs. County. This may Cartefy that the Bearer Hereof a Negro man named Ben is a free Negro as he formerly belonged to Mr. Jonathan Sharwod Deceased who having Many Slaves and no Children alive not Desiering his Slaves Should Serve another Master Did in his will Generously give them freedom. Which if

Disputed may be found on Record in the Court of the Said County aforsaid and the afore named Negro Man having a Desier to travel to Virginia to Seek better imployment we the Subscriber Do Cartify that the Said Negro is a free man has Ever Sence his working for himself behaved very honest therefore we the Subscribers Do Recomend the Said negro to Such Gentlemen as Shall imploy him. Witness our hands this 21 Janay. 1784.

Richard Malliest

Certificate of freedom, January 21, 1784, Chowan County, Miscellaneous Records, Slave Records, State Archives, Office of Archives and History, Raleigh.

CHAPTER XI.

An Act to Prevent the Stealing of Slaves or by Violation, Seduction or any other Means, taking or conveying away any slave or slaves, the property of another; and for other purposes therein mentioned.

I. Whereas, it is necessary that the promiscuous practice of stealing or other ways carrying away slaves the property of others, as also of stealing and carrying off free negroes and mulattoes with an intention to sell and appropriate the same, should be discouraged by a law with additional penalties.

II. Be it enacted by the General Assembly and by the authority of the same, that any person or persons who shall hereafter steal or shall by violence, seduction or any other means, take or convey away any slave or slaves, the property of another, with an intention to sell or dispose of to another or appropriate to their own use such slave or slaves, or who shall hereafter by violence or any other means, take or convey any free negro or free negroes or persons of mixed blood, out of this State to another, with an intention to sell or dispose of such free Negro or free negroes or persons of mixed blood, and being thereof legally convicted or shall upon his arraignment peremptorily challenge more than thirty five jurors, or shall stand mute, shall be judged guilty of Felony and shall suffer death without benefit of Clergy.

Laws, 1778, in Clark, *State Records*, XXIV:220.

SOURCES CITED

Admiralty Papers, British Records. North Carolina State Archives, Office of Archives and History, Raleigh.

Americanus, Scotus. "Informations Concerning the Province of North Carolina, Etc." in "Some North Carolina Tracts of the Eighteenth Century," edited by William K. Boyd. *North Carolina Historical Review* 3 (October 1926): 591-621.

Audit Office Papers, British Records. North Carolina State Archives, Office of Archives and History, Raleigh.

Bertie County, Minutes of the Court of Pleas and Quarter Sessions. North Carolina State Archives, Office of Archives and History, Raleigh.

Bertie County, Miscellaneous Records, Slave Records. North Carolina State Archives, Office of Archives and History, Raleigh.

Boyd, William K., ed. *William Byrd's Histories of the Dividing Line Betwixt Virginia and North Carolina.* Raleigh: North Carolina Historical Commission, 1929.

Brickell, John. *The Natural History of North Carolina.* 1737. Reprint. Murfreesboro, N.C.: Johnson Publishing Co., 1968.

Cain, Robert J., ed. *The Church of England in North Carolina: Documents, 1699-1741.* Volume X of *The Colonial Records of North Carolina [Second Series].* Raleigh: Division of Archives and History, Department of Cultural Resources [projected multivolume series, 1963-], 1999.

Cape Fear Mercury (Wilmington).

Carroll, Grady L., ed. *Francis Asbury in North Carolina: The North Carolina Portions of the Journal of Francis Asbury.* Nashville, Tenn.: Parthenon Press, 1964.

Chatham Furnace Papers. Southern Historical Collection, Manuscripts Department, Wilson Library, University of North Carolina at Chapel Hill.

Chowan County, Minutes of the Court of Pleas and Quarter Sessions. North Carolina State Archives, Office of Archives and History, Raleigh.

Chowan County, Miscellaneous Records, Slave Records. North Carolina State Archives, Office of Archives and History, Raleigh.

Clark, Walter, ed. *The State Records of North Carolina.* 16 vols. (11-26) Raleigh: State of North Carolina, 1895-1906.

Commager, Henry Steele, ed. *Documents of American History.* 2 vols., 7th ed. New York: Appleton-Century-Crofts, 1963.

Commerce of Rhode Island, 1726-1800, Volume I, *1726-1774.* In *Collections of the Massachusetts Historical Society,* 7th ser., Volume IX. Boston: the society, 1914.

Commissioners' Minutes, Town of New Bern. North Carolina State Archives, Office of Archives and History, Raleigh.

Cooper, Thomas, David J. McCord, and successive secretaries of state, eds. *The Statutes at Large of South Carolina.* 22 vols. Columbia, S.C.: A. S. Johnston, 1836-1898.

Craven County, Minutes of the Court of Pleas and Quarter Sessions. North Carolina State Archives, Office of Archives and History, Raleigh.

Cumberland County, Minutes of the Court of Pleas and Quarter Sessions. North Carolina State Archives, Office of Archives and History, Raleigh.

Donnan, Elizabeth, ed. *Documents Illustrative of the History of the Slave Trade to America.* 4 vols. 1931. Reprint. New York: Octagon Books, 1965.

Fries, Adelaide L. et al., eds. *Records of the Moravians in North Carolina.* 12 vols. to date. Raleigh: North Carolina Historical Commission, 1922-.

General Assembly Session Records, Colonial (Upper and Lower House). North Carolina State Archives, Office of Archives and History, Raleigh.

Granville County, Miscellaneous Records, Civil Actions Concerning Slaves and Free Persons of Color. North Carolina State Archives, Office of Archives and History, Raleigh.

Granville County, Miscellaneous Records, Miscellaneous Records of Slaves and Free Persons of Color. North Carolina State Archives, Office of Archives and History, Raleigh.

Grimes, J. Bryan, comp. *North Carolina Wills and Inventories.* Raleigh: Edwards & Broughton Printing Co., 1912.

Hathaway, James Robert Bent, ed. *North Carolina Historical and Genealogical Register.* 3 vols. Edenton: N.p., 1900-1903.

Hayes Papers. Southern Historical Collection, Manuscripts Department, Wilson Library, University of North Carolina at Chapel Hill.

Hening, William Waller, ed. *The Statutes at Large; Being a Collection of All the Laws of Virginia.* 13 vols., 2d ed. Philadelphia: the editor, by Thomas Desilver, 1820-1823.

Higginbotham, Don, ed. *The Papers of James Iredell.* Vol 2, *1778-1783.* Raleigh: Division of Archives and History, Department of Cultural Resources, 1976.

Higginbotham, Don and William S. Price Jr. "Was It Murder for a White Man to Kill a Slave? Chief Justice Martin Howard Condemns the Peculiar Institution in North Carolina." *William and Mary Quarterly*, 3d ser., 36 (October 1979): 593-601.

Howe, Mark A. De Wolfe, ed. "Journal of Josiah Quincy, Junior, 1773." *Proceedings of the Massachusetts Historical Society* 49 (June 1916): 424-481.

Hyde County, Minutes of the Court of Pleas and Quarter Sessions. North Carolina State Archives, Office of Archives and History, Raleigh.

Johnston, Hugh Buckner, ed. "The Journal of Ebenezer Hazard in North Carolina, 1777 and 1778." *North Carolina Historical Review* 36 (July 1959): 358-381.

Johnston County, Miscellaneous Records, Special Court for the Trial of Negroes. North Carolina State Archives, Office of Archives and History, Raleigh.

"The Journal of James Auld, 1765-1770." *Publications of the Southern History Association* 8 (July 1904): 253-268.

Keith, Alice Barnwell, ed. *The John Gray Blount Papers.* Vol. 1, *1764-1789.* Raleigh: Division of Archives and History, Department of Cultural Resources, 1952.

Laws of the State of North-Carolina. Newbern: Arnett & Hodge, Printers to the State, 1786-1836.

Lemmon, Sarah McCulloh, ed. *The Pettigrew Papers*. 2 vols. to date. Raleigh: Division of Archives and History, Department of Cultural Resources, 1971-.

Lennon, Donald R. and Ida B. Kellam, eds. *The Wilmington Town Book, 1743-1778*. Raleigh: Division of Archives and History, Department of Cultural Resources, 1973.

McAllister Papers. Southern Historical Collection, Manuscripts Department, Wilson Library, University of North Carolina at Chapel Hill.

McEachern, Leora H. and Isabel M. Williams, eds. *Wilmington-New Hanover Safety Committee Minutes, 1774-1776*. Wilmington, N.C.: Wilmington-New Hanover County American Revolution Bi-Centennial Association, 1974.

New Bern District Superior Court, Criminal Action Papers. North Carolina State Archives, Office of Archives and History, Raleigh.

New Hanover County, Minutes of the Court of Pleas and Quarter Sessions. North Carolina State Archives, Office of Archives and History, Raleigh.

New Hanover County, Miscellaneous Records, Coroners' Inquests. North Carolina State Archives, Office of Archives and History, Raleigh.

New Hanover County, Miscellaneous Records, Records of Slaves and Free Persons of Color, Emancipation Records. North Carolina State Archives, Office of Archives and History, Raleigh.

Newsome, Albert R., ed. "A British Orderly Book, 1780-1781." *North Carolina Historical Review* 9 (July 1932): 273-298.

North Carolina Gazette (New Bern).

North Carolina Magazine; or, Universal Intelligencer (New Bern).

Onslow County, Minutes of the Court of Pleas and Quarter Sessions. North Carolina State Archives, Office of Archives and History, Raleigh.

Onslow County, Miscellaneous Records, Slave (Bills of Sale). North Carolina State Archives, Office of Archives and History, Raleigh.

Onslow County, Miscellaneous Records, Slave (Civil Actions Concerning). North Carolina State Archives, Office of Archives and History, Raleigh.

Onslow County, Miscellaneous Records, Slave (Criminal Actions Concerning). North Carolina State Archives, Office of Archives and History, Raleigh.

Parker, Freddie L., ed. *Stealing a Little Freedom: Advertisements for Slave Runaways in North Carolina, 1791-1840*. New York: Garland Publishing Co., 1994.

Parker, Mattie Erma Edwards, ed. *North Carolina Charters and Constitutions, 1578-1698*. Volume I of *The Colonial Records of North Carolina* [*Second Series*]. Raleigh: Division of Archives and History, Department of Cultural Resources [projected multivolume series 1963-], 1963.

_____, ed. *North Carolina Higher-Court Records, 1670-1696*. Volume II of *The Colonial Records of North Carolina* [*Second Series*]. Raleigh: Division of Archives and History, Department of Cultural Resources [projected multivolume series, 1963-], 1968.

_____, ed. *North Carolina Higher-Court Records, 1697-1701*. Volume III of *The Colonial Records of North Carolina* [*Second Series*]. Raleigh: Division of Archives and History, Department of Cultural Resources [projected multivolume series, 1963-], 1971.

Pasquotank County, Minutes of the Court of Pleas and Quarter Sessions. North Carolina State Archives, Office of Archives and History, Raleigh.

Pasquotank County, Miscellaneous Records, Records of Slaves and Free Persons of Color, Bonds and Petitions to Free Slaves. North Carolina State Archives, Office of Archives and History, Raleigh.

Pasquotank County, Miscellaneous Records, Records of Slaves and Free Persons of Color, Court Actions Involving Slaves. North Carolina State Archives, Offices of Archives and History, Raleigh.

Pennsylvania Gazette (Philadelphia).

Perquimans County, Miscellaneous Records, Slave Records, Civil and Criminal Cases. North Carolina State Archives, Office of Archives and History, Raleigh.

Perquimans County, Miscellaneous Records, Slave Records, Miscellaneous Slave Papers. North Carolina State Archives, Office of Archives and History, Raleigh.

Perquimans County, Miscellaneous Records, Slave Records, Petitions for Emancipation. North Carolina State Archives, Office of Archives and History, Raleigh.

Powell, William S., ed. "Tryon's 'Book' on North Carolina." *North Carolina Historical Review* 34 (July 1957): 406-415.

Price, William S. Jr., ed. *North Carolina Higher-Court Records, 1702-1708*. Volume IV of *The Colonial Records of North Carolina* [*Second Series*]. Raleigh: Division of Archives and History, Department of Cultural Resources [projected multivolume series, 1963-], 1974.

_____, ed. *North Carolina Higher-Court Records, 1709-1723*. Volume V of *The Colonial Records of North Carolina* [*Second Series*]. Raleigh: Division of Archives and History, Department of Cultural Resources [projected multivolume series, 1963-], 1977.

Rodman, Lida Tunstall, ed. *Journal of a Tour to North Carolina by William Attmore*. Chapel Hill: James Sprunt Historical Publications, 1922.

Rowan County, Minutes of the Court of Pleas and Quarter Sessions. North Carolina State Archives, Office of Archives and History, Raleigh.

Saunders, William L., ed. *The Colonial Records of North Carolina*. 10 vols. Raleigh: State of North Carolina, 1886-1890.

Schaw, Janet. *Journal of a Lady of Quality; Being the Narrative of a Journey from Scotland to the West Indies, North Carolina, and Portugal, in the Years 1774 and 1775*. Edited by Evangeline W. Andrews and Charles M. Andrews. New Haven: Yale University Press, 1921.

Schoepf, Johann David. *Travels in the Confederation, 1783-1784*. 2 vols. Translated and edited by Alfred J. Morrison. Philadelphia: W. J. Campbell, 1911.

Schütz, Géza, ed. "Additions to the History of the Swiss Colonization Projects in Carolina." *North Carolina Historical Review* 10 (April 1933): 133-141.

Slave Collection. North Carolina State Archives, Office of Archives and History, Raleigh.

Smyth, John F. D. *A Tour in the United States of America.* 2 vols. 1784. Reprint. New York: Arno Press, 1968.

State Gazette of North Carolina (Edenton).

State Gazette of North Carolina (New Bern).

Tiffany, Nina Moore, ed. *Letters of James Murray, Loyalist.* Boston: the editor, 1901.

Van Horne, John C., ed. *Religious Philanthropy and Colonial Slavery: The American Correspondence of the Associates of Dr. Bray, 1717-1777.* Urbana: University of Illinois Press, 1985.

Virginia Gazette (Williamsburg: Parks).

Virginia Gazette (Williamsburg: Purdie and Dixon).

Virginia Gazette (Williamsburg: Rind).

Wake County, Minutes of the Court of Pleas and Quarter Sessions. North Carolina State Archives, Office of Archives and History, Raleigh.

Watson, Winslow C., ed. *Men and Times of the Revolution; or, Memoirs of Elkanah Watson.* New York: Dana and Co., 1856.

"William Logan's Journal of a Journey to Georgia, 1745." *Pennsylvania Magazine of History and Biography* 36 (1912): 1-16.

Wilmington Centinel, and General Advertiser.

Wright, Louis B. and Marion Tinling, eds. *Quebec to Carolina in 1785-1786. Being the Travel Diary and Observations of Robert Hunter, Jr., a Young Methodist of London.* San Marino, California: Huntington Library, 1943.

Index

Abberdeen (fled to HMS *Scorpion*), 99

Abraham (fled to HMS *Scorpion*), 99

Abraham (slave of John Kennedy), 90-91, 92

Act of Assembly (N.C.): bars slaves from keeping houses, 143; and Beaufort County, 115; and Bladen County, 115; and Bute County, 28; on carrying of weapons by slaves, 64-65, 66, 88-89, 106, 121, 124; and Chatham County, 28; compensates owners of outlawed, executed slaves, 112-113, 113-114, 115; and Cumberland County, 115; and Edenton, 138-139, 141-142; and Edgecombe County, 28; on emancipation, 28-30, 32-34, 35-36, 145, 147, 148, 149-150; on enslavement of free blacks, mulattoes, 161-162, 164; on entertainment of slaves, 67, 140; and Fayetteville, 141-142; free blacks, mulattoes mentioned in, 51, 64, 68, 119, 124, 129, 131, 145, 147; and Granville County, 28, 115; and Halifax County, 28, 115; on harboring of runaway slaves, servants, 61, 67; on herding livestock, 42; on hiring-out of slaves, 51, 124, 129, 140, 141-142; on hunting by slaves, 64-65; on importation of slaves, 6, 7, 8-9, 10, 129, 131, 147; on interracial marriage, union, 73, 74-75, 76-77, 153, 154-155; on killing slaves, 117-119; on legal proceedings, and slaves, 102, 106, 107, 117-118, 119-120; on livestock-keeping, by slaves, 27, 28; and marriage of slaves, 41, 42; and Northampton County, 28; and Orange County, 10, 28; and Perquimans County, 115; and Pitt County, 115; on pilots, ports, 21-22, 23-24; precedent for, set by Va., S.C., xii, 73-74, 89-90, 93-95, 106-107; requires slaves to carry passes, 42, 63, 64, 88-89, 121, 124, 129; restricts slave meetings, gatherings, 50, 51-52, 67, 136; on runaway slaves, 29, 61, 67, 88-89, 90, 91, 93, 94-95; on servants and slaves, (1699), 61, (1705/6), 61-62, (1715), 28, 29, 61, 63, 67, 68-69, 73, 74, 88-89, 90, 107, 112-113, (1741), 28, 29, 61, 64-65, 76, 93, 94-95, 96, 141-142, 161-162, (1753), 65, 112, 113, 121, 123, (1758), 112, 113-114, (1779), 123-124, (1785), 141-142; on slave insurrections, 30, 35-36, 96, 131-132, 136; and slave patrols, 51, 121-122, 123-125, 126, 128, 129, 131-132; and slaveholders, 51-52, 112-113, 113-114, 115, 124, 129, 141-142; on theft of slaves, 86, 164; on tobacco cultivation by slaves, 27, 28; on toll books, 42; on trafficking with slaves, 61-62, 68-69, 70-71, 138-139; and Wake County, 28; and Washington, 141-142; and Wilmington, 136, 141-142, 143. *See also* Slave code

Act of Assembly (S.C.), xii, 71, 122

Act of Assembly (Va.): exempts free blacks, mulattoes, from payment

GeeK Squad.com

Geeks on call.com